Mãe Luíza
Building Optimism

Mãe Luíza
Building Optimism

Edited by
Ion de Andrade
Tomislav Dushanov
Nicole Miescher
Lars Müller

Paulo Lins
Creating a New Sun

Lars Müller Publishers

Paulo Lins

Creating a New Sun

Translated by Ángel Gurría-Quintana

Preface

The first part of this book is a work of fiction but is based on the harsh reality of Brazil's poorest neighborhoods and favelas, afflicted, since their inception, by a criminal social inequality. From the moment it enters the era of Father Sabino Gentili, the narrative is based on true events.

The best position anyone can find themselves in is being able to help others without expecting anything in return. There are many ways to offer help: helping oneself to show more solidarity; helping someone else, whether personally, or by allowing them to be socially included; helping the planet so that we have a better quality of life and can enjoy nature's gifts.

Helping someone should not be a one-off act that will solve their problem only temporarily. To help is to make them self-sufficient so that they may never again need help, so that they may carry on unassisted for the rest of their lives, in full control and therefore able to help others who also need to be helped.

Social equality is not something we should have to fight for. Any individual should naturally feel included in society, by the simple fact of being born. But wealth is unequally distributed between nations, states, cities and societies. That is why the fight for a fairer world must come from within all people of goodwill.

For years I have been socially included. I was helped by two teachers who, alongside their regular school classes, took their students to the theatre, to musicals, and welcomed them into their own homes, on weekends and during the holidays, reinforcing what they taught at school and preparing them for public sector job applications and university entrance exams. Those women were able to break the historical inevitability of my becoming one more among the excluded because I am black, and the son of migrants from the Northeast, in a country with one of the highest inequality rates in the world, where slavery lasted longer and kept more human beings in shackles than anywhere else on the planet.

Today I am a graduate in Modern Languages, I am a writer, I work in film and television thanks to the people of good will who worked and fought for social justice, as do all those people I met in Mãe Luíza.

I was asked to write this book – with its happy ending – about how we can help others restore, reclaim or even acquire their human rights.

The first part tells the story of people who sought refuge from droughts and arrived in Natal seeking better lives. Initially they lived on the streets, begged to kill their hunger, and built a favela as the only way to house themselves.

In the early days of the Mãe Luíza favela, hunger haunted families' daily lives, and diseases blighted the bodies of people of all ages. Infant mortality was high, as was the number of elderly living in insalubrious conditions. Public schools were under-resourced, teachers were poorly paid and unable to offer a good education, and crime welcomed the young into its fold. This was life without any form of state support – the criminal abandonment of the excluded to whom, to this day, authorities and politicians deny any human right.

The second part shows how social inclusion initiatives carried out by people inside and outside of Brazil transformed the Mãe Luíza favela into the *bairro* Mãe Luíza – the Mãe Luíza neighborhood.

This book proves that we can live with dignity in a just and equal society by working and investing in what is best in this world: human beings.

Paulo Lins

Among all things, I learned to like only the moonless nights, because there is nothing to reflect your light. I hate it when you look down at me, when you wrap yourself around me, when you rule over everything with your king-of-the-world gaze, debasing what is mine.

Why should I care that for some you are the bringer of beauty, the light of all paths, the cure for darkness, if you are the cause of all ills for my family, for the roads I travel, for the animals that clothe me, that protect me, that are loyal to me, that kill my hunger. You reign hazily over my air. You are a master of death and misery, a bulwark of pain, a harbinger of emptiness.

Here are my tears, what little water I still have left, for you to turn into water vapor, into nothing, like those rivers whose legs you break, preventing them from fulfilling their fate of dying in the ocean. They succumb in their youth, deprived of the passage they may have followed, producing flowers, spreading riches, generating forests.

Only rocks remain, instead of fruit. The grasslands are cemeteries lined with cadavers.

I would like to live at the bottom of the sea, on a snow-covered mountaintop, anywhere you cannot reach. From here, where I am now, I can see the cattle's carcasses, your eyes' evil spreading over what was once a plantation. I look at the empty well, the dead trees, your rays like a disease infesting humans. How many have died because of you? How many have not been born?

I was born in this place, at a time when rain still fell from time to time, in the winter, kissing the faces of the old, caressing the cattle's back, bringing color to the flowers. But then you came, sowing the night with moonlight and stars, like a false happiness that brings no water, it comes without the delight of dew, without the damp breeze to nuzzle us, without the hope of keeping you far away forever.

You are the one that perishes and is reborn to kill. Dawn is the proclaimed despair. The blue that encloses you is a metaphor for hell.

Sun, you are the assassin that slays as it shines.

José went to the well before the accursed sun had risen. He found Valdir with the bucket full of mud. There was no more water. The solution was to dig another well close to the source of the last river to dry up. José did not believe they would find even the smallest trickle of water in that area. They both walked in silence, holding the empty bucket. There would not even be enough water to cook that day.

Oswaldo and Joana went to meet them. News of the well drying up brought tears to the woman's eyes. There would be no drinking water. There was no food left over from the previous day. José had a small amount of water at home. At least the children would not be thirsty.

When they got back to the small village, some of the few neighbors were walking towards the well.

"You might as well turn back, the well's dried up. It's just mud, not even good for filtering. If we don't leave this place today, we'll die of thirst," Valdir said.

Joana looked up at the sky, arms open, and begged, with tears welling in her eyes:

"Dear God, just a few drops of rain, I beg you in the name of Jesus."

"God is making us go to São Paulo, Rio de Janeiro or even Natal." said Lúcia, José's wife. This place here, it's been taken over by the devil. He must be a friend of the sun. No, not a friend. It, the sun, is the devil."

"Stop that, Lúcia. Let's go to the chapel and pray. Maybe God will hear our prayers."

"Not even the priest, who used to come every Sunday, is there. The chapel is falling to pieces. The pastor, too, stopped coming the moment that the colonel stopped showing up. The tithes stopped, and suddenly the blood of Christ lost its power. God wants us to be strong and get out of this place like they did. Jesus gave us the intelligence to apply our own free will."

"Lúcia, do you want to abandon our home, our land? Our dead, who are buried here? My place is where my dead are."

"No, José, I just don't want to die of thirst. Don't you understand?"

"Valdir and I are going to find water. There must be a pool of river water that the sun hasn't dried up yet."

"If you don't find the water, José, we'll die, you hear me? We'll die of thirst! I'm leaving now. We have enough water for one more day, for everyone. Tomorrow it's all gone."

The argument went on for a little longer, everyone agreed with Lúcia. They went home to pack the few clothes they possessed, their old photographs, bibles, old birthday and Christmas gifts. They would leave at night. If they travelled by day, they would die from the heat.

The families packed their belongings, which did not amount to much. In the afternoon they would go to the cemetery to say farewell to their dead. At José and Lúcia's house there was a quarrel with Fefedo. Among the children he was the most attached to the place, and unlike his sisters Regina and Neuza, and his younger brother Chico, said he would never leave. He was scared of the big city, he refused to go to the cemetery to say farewell to the dead, he wanted to be buried near them. Calmly, Lúcia tried to persuade her son to leave. He was only 18, he might spend only a short time in Natal. When the rains returned, the family would come back too. Fefedo did not budge. She talked and talked and talked, but the boy, stony-faced, sat in a corner saying that he did not want to leave.

They left him alone for a while. By night-time he would have changed his mind. Lúcia thought that it would be easy to say good-bye to the dead, but it was not. To leave that sacred space was like abandoning all her history, letting go of the ties that bound her to those loved ones. It had been a long time since there were even any flowers to decorate the graves. The bones, without any moisture to keep them for longer, had turned to dust. The crying lasted until night started falling, and then they hastily got on the road to Natal. They had to move fast and arrive at Monte Alegre, where they might find drinking water.

Fefedo took a long time to be persuaded. He wanted to stay behind and be buried with the grandparents, cousins and uncles lost to the dried-up life he did not want to abandon. After a lot of talking with Lúcia and José, he got up to start the trek towards the capital alongside his family and neighbors.

They walked past the fazenda's abandoned manor house, everything was falling apart with rot and decay. The owner had left with his family, saying that the sun was the devil's work and that God had lost his battle over that limitless blue patch of sky.

The family had already been walking for some time when Lúcia told her husband that her period was very late. She was sure she was expecting another child. They embraced, smiling, thanking God because the child that was coming would not know the drought. Suddenly Fefedo turned back in a rush, crying out that he had forgotten something. His parents shouted at him to come back, but the boy paid no attention. He ran into the church, picked up the images of Our Lady of Aparecida and of Saint Joseph carrying the Child Jesus, and then continued the journey with his parents. Lúcia kissed him. They left the place behind without the smallest shred of hope. They were following a dry riverbed, hoping that there might be a small pool of water on what was once the river's watery course.

Seven-year-old Chico was excited, happy about the new life that lay ahead. He could not understand why his brother was so attached to that place that only foreshadowed hunger, thirst and death. In the big city he would go to school, his father would find a job, they would live in a house with running water in the kitchen, an inside toilet, bedrooms and a living room, like at the fazenda's big house.

Fefedo's heart was simple. For him the greater misfortune was not the drought, but having to abandon his land. He was certain that one day the rain would return, and they would once again find water in that place that cradled him. He did not like big cities, too many people crowded together, too many cars coming and going. Every time he had been to the city with his father, he had pleaded to leave soon. He remembered how, in the place where he was born, whenever he needed to unwind he simply walked out into the fields, alone with the universe, with his animals, in the knowledge that he would be happy forever. His eyes brimmed with shallow tears. That was the place where his grandparents held him for the very last time.

They walked in silence through the night. By the time the sun came out, dry and cracked mud was already skinning their feet, their heels were heavy with blood. Fefedo carried Chico on his shoulders, the parrot was on the back of the dog, which every now and then stopped to lick the remains of a dead animal with its black tongue. At one point the dog noticed a live guinea pig playing dead to stay alive. Baleia was not fooled: she swiftly snatched the animal and brought it for José to cut open, roast over a fire and split between the children. Baleia licked the blood that dripped on the hot earth and felt satisfied. The parrot simply said: "Finally."

They continued their journey.

Soon they found a pool of briny water. The liquid left traces of dirt as it slid down their throats, yet it quenched the thirst that spread through the migrants' bodies.

They arrived in Natal at the break of dawn after a night of walking. At the city's entrance they noted the poverty of people living in the outskirts. Lúcia prayed that she would not die in a place such as that, and that José would soon find a job as a house painter.

It was he who had painted the houses of the fazenda where they lived, and he re-painted them every year for the end-of-year festivities. He had learned the trade as a child with his father, the late Seu José. Lúcia was going to work as a maid. There was no shortage of work in rich people's houses. She might even find a job before her husband, especially because she did not need a contract for that kind of work. She would work at least until the fifth month of her pregnancy.

They came across a modest bakery, already open. With what little money they had, the ten grown-ups and eight children were able to drink water and eat bread with mortadella sausage. The baker, taking pity on the group's sickly appearance, offered them cake, refreshments, soft drinks and sweets for the children. He prayed to God that they might cross paths with someone who would help them. Feeling more optimistic, the group continued walking towards the city. The parrot was saying that it wanted happiness and nothing else.

José thought it might be best to find their way to a rich neighborhood, where it would be easier to beg for money to eat and drink. Perhaps a neighborhood near the beach, so they could sleep on the sand, under the open sky. If they could not find somewhere to have a shower or bath, they could wash themselves in the sea and get rid of the earth that coated their skin. Saltwater cures the body's wounds, it unclogs the nose. Despite the salt, it is water.

The people they came across, even the ones who avoided them because of their appearance or their odor, gave them small change. With the little money they collected they ate sandwiches and drank water.

Their first night by the ocean was like sleeping in a luxury hotel. The sound of the waves was music to Fefedo's ears, and he wondered why there were no freshwater oceans elsewhere. Also, why were his parents so poor? Why was there no water in the place they came from? Why had he not been born in the capital, and grown used to living there from his childhood? Why be born, anyway, if life was so hard? Why did God not make all men equal? Why did people not have the same right to a life of riches?

The other migrants were already asleep when Fefedo noticed three policemen, batons in hand, approaching them at speed. Once again he queried the heavens: was it God who had sent those cops?

Fearful, he cried out to his father, but José, exhausted, did not even budge. Fefedo was going to call out to his mother by the time the policemen were upon them, shouting and kicking.

Lúcia tried to protect the children. As they hit the men, the cops shouted that they had told them sleeping on the beach was forbidden. The residents of that rich neighborhood did not want rough sleepers on their streets or on the beach. One of them had gone out to do some early morning exercise, had seen the migrants making themselves comfortable on the sand and had told the police that there was a gang of tramps. They were surely going to mug passersby.

The travelers explained that they had only recently arrived, that they were from Lagoa Salgada and were escaping the drought. The policemen were not listening. Men, women and children were shoved, hit with batons and kicked. Fefedo was the only one of the children who did not cry. He looked hard into the eyes of the attackers without saying a word, he wanted to remember their faces. Baleia barked, she bit the leg of one of the cops so hard that she drew blood, and then ran off, fleeing the other policemen's gunshots. The parrot flew silently above the group.

The new arrivals hurried back onto the streets, moving away from the beach. One of the policemen had warned them that, if they ever returned, he would kill them all. He added that he was going to track down that damn dog that almost tore his friend's leg off.

José argued that, in large cities, the city center is deserted at night, so they followed the signs that pointed them in that direction.

When they arrived, they found many people sleeping under the shop awnings, but they could not make themselves at home yet. Every spot was precisely marked out. There were people who lived very far away and slept in the city center from Monday to Friday to avoid losing hours of sleep on public transport; there were those who had been expelled from their communities by gang leaders; the truly homeless; criminals recently released from prison with nowhere to go; children abandoned to God's mercy; and the old, abandoned by their children. All lived together around the main square, but each group in its own designated place.

After some time, they found some floorspace on which to lay their bodies down in a building site near the main square. They knew they would have to get up early. Baleia reappeared with her tongue hanging out, her muzzle dirty with blood from the guard's leg. Then the parrot landed next to Fefedo, who was still fuming with rage as he carried Chico, seemingly happy in his sleep.

They all fell asleep soon, apart from Fefedo, who remained awake and attentive to the movements on the street. On the other side of the square, he could see the prostitutes coming and going. Every minute a car would pull up to one of them, and she would talk to the driver. Some would get into the cars, which then drove off at speed. Others waited to negotiate their terms.

There were boys smoking and selling weed, and passing paper wraps filled with cocaine on to buyers who arrived on foot, by car and by motorcycle.

What most surprised Fefedo was seeing policemen arrive to collect money from the man who loitered with the prostitutes and from the boys selling drugs. They all seemed to be well acquainted with one another, they spoke with an easy familiarity. He was astonished to see the men in uniform smoking weed, snorting cocaine and laughing with the dealers. He did not understand what exactly was happening in that square, but he could guess from the television news he watched back at the fazenda.

At seven o'clock in the morning the shop owners started arriving, as did their security guards and employees. The family moved to the center of the square. They agreed that they should not stay together because they might draw attention to themselves. Two grown-ups would have to stay with the children in a safe spot, begging for money, while the others tried to find jobs somewhere nearby in the city center. At night they would meet in the same place to sleep. Fefedo, deprived of sleep, could not stay awake. He found a tree and fell asleep beneath it.

Oswaldo and Joana remained in the square with the children. Lúcia made her way to the rich neighborhood to try to find a job as a maid. José and the other men stayed at the building site where they had spent the night. The site's foreman, who had also escaped the drought, welcomed them. Only José got work as a painter. He was delighted to be given an overall, boots and a hard hat, and to jump straight into the job. The rest of the men went in search of other building sites that the foreman had recommended.

Things were tougher for the women that day. With their ragged clothes, their body odor and their unhealthy aspect, building porters refused to even speak to them. When they rang the doorbells at some of the richer homes, the ladies of the house, assuming the women were begging for money, shut their doors and shouted from inside that they had nothing to give them.

But the women did not give up. Sometimes they were lucky enough to come across a good-hearted person who, even without giving them a job, offered them water and some food. They ate part of it and saved the rest for the children. They kept trying to find work until the early evening and then returned to the square.

Fefedo was still sleeping under a tree. Happiness spread through the group when José returned and announced that the foreman had allowed all of them to wash themselves and wash their clothes at the building site. It was the first time they were able to do that since they left Lagoa Salgada. Their skin was filthy, dirt-crusted and sun-cracked. It was their happiest night for a long time.

Water is the mistress of all happiness. In the shape of tears, it clears away the hurt caused by heartbreak and by the accumulation of sadness. Water rekindles happiness under the sun, because there will always be a seed on the ground in need of it. In the form of a river, water fills life with the hope of reaching the sea. In a glass, it reinvigorates. In the form of rain, it makes all creatures joyful. Those who do not have it become wretched when they are forced to leave behind their land, their churches, their dead.

In the form of a jet, the water from the hose covers Fefedo's body and reanimates his fury, his desire to do whatever needs to be done to make life more bearable. Even if, in a very near future, that means killing a few unfortunates who might cross his path. It's eat or be eaten. Where there is no water, violence is the main currency. He thinks that, in order to be happy, a man should not have to depend on anything essential, like food, or a house, or water. If we did not depend on those things there would be no evil, no greed, no envy or theft.

Fefedo washed himself in a hurry. He put on his clothes and hurried over to the square. Chico wanted to be carried by him, cuddled, played with, made safe.

Around the square, workers were leaving their jobs, people were eating in the snack counters and the few bars. Fefedo walked around the square scoffing some of the food brought back by the women. Then he walked around the nearby streets trying to take it all in, paying attention to even the smallest details. That is what he did when he was working the fields. He knew about everything and everyone, at all times of the day. Now he wanted to know every detail about the nightlife, the comings and goings of the prostitutes, the crooks, the drug pushers, the users and, above all, the policemen.

He lied down with Chico is his arms, waiting for the night workers to show up. When everyone was asleep, he placed his brother on top of his father, who was sleeping heavily, and walked to the other side of the square.

He loitered near the drug pushers until someone said:

"Looking for something?"

"Money."

"What will you do to get it?"

"Whatever I have to."

"That's the spirit. Where are you from?"

"I've escaped the drought."

"You hungry?"

"Hungry and thirsty."

"Go to the bar over there, ask for a sandwich and a soft drink, and tell them to put it on Marçal Aquino's tab."

Fefedo went to the bar and came back shortly eating a sausage sandwich.

"Just sit there and watch. I like you. You have a good attitude."

The boy sat down and looked over at the place where Marçal and his partners sold weed and the cocaine. He observed the prostitutes gathering in a corner, waiting for their customers.

There, in that other part of the city center, there were many homeless people. They included other migrants escaping the droughts, drunks, the unemployed, the mentally ill, alcoholics, former prisoners, the wretched of all sorts.

Local business owners and residents regularly complained to the authorities about the homeless, who in their eyes were all criminals. Often the police arrived to expel those unfortunates, beating them up and shooting into the air. Every now and then they shot one of the poor devils at close range, claiming to have been returning fire.

The migrants preferred to sleep around the square because there were more awnings to stay under, more passing drivers to sell things to at traffic lights, more passersby to ask for money, places to wash and snack counters to find leftover food. That square was also the gathering point for the city's educated youth, who did not mind mixing with the regulars in those seedy bars, where everyone was left wing. The migrants did not understand why things were calmer there, but were certain that they would not be bothered, and that seemed enough.

With so many complaints being lodged by local residents and business owners, the mayor, Djalma Maranhão, had decided to see for himself the state in which those homeless people were living. He had visited another part of the city, and had been shocked and saddened by what he saw. Not knowing what to offer, he had told the people that there was some scrubland near a well over by the dunes. The land belonged to the city, but people would be able to live on it for free. They could build their own houses, and get by, and later he would personally make sure that they became the lawful owners of the properties.

Early the next morning a crowd of poor migrants had made its way towards that land, which was difficult to reach because it was all sand and scrub. The police had been unsure of what to do when they saw so many wretched souls walking in the same direction. They tried to disperse the group by beating them up and shooting into the air. Only when the mayor showed up to accompany the group had the procession been able to continue its journey in peace.

But, when they got to the place, nobody had wanted to stay in that dense scrubland, infested with snakes and scorpions. That was no place for humans to live. Better to remain in the city, where it was easier to get water and food.

Pedro, one of the homeless, had looked at Luíza, his wife, who understood what the look meant and nodded her agreement. The people had started leaving, and when they looked back they saw that the couple was not moving. Pedro said that he and his wife would stay in that place. If Djalma Maranhão had offered them the land, that was where they intended to remain. Enough of the sadness of sleeping under awnings, on dirty streets in the city center.

"You have to be a big man to drag your woman to a place like this," one of the other homeless people said.

"He is a big man, that's why I'm with him," Dona Luíza replied, before adding: "And I'm a big woman!"

The crowd left and "Big Man" Pedro looked around. He told his wife to wait near the beach while he got a pickaxe, a spade and a machete. He walked towards a building site, and explained his situation to the foreman, who loaned him the tools. Pedro returned quickly. He took Luíza's hand, and the couple walked into the dense scrub.

"The further in we go, the better."

They had filled their bellies with water. Then, guided by the sunlight, which sometimes disappeared behind the treetops, they made their way with effort into that new place. She was behind him carrying the pickaxe and he walked ahead with the machete and the spade, cutting a trail through the undergrowth. They struck the foliage to scare off the snakes and the scorpions. They walked over a flat plain for almost two hours, and then climbed one kilometer further until they could see the ocean.

It was there, deep inside the scrubland, that "Big Man" Pedro cleared the ground, saving the tree trunks and branches to build his hut later on. When night started to fall, they returned to the city center to beg for money, to eat and to sleep.

On it went for 30 days, until they had built a wattle-and-daub hut with two bedrooms, a dining area and a kitchen. It was not possible to dig a well in that spot, so Pedro wandered further into the scrub, but found no streams or waterfalls. They had to beg for money, trying to get enough to buy working tools and some metal drums to store water so they could build a huge vegetable garden, a large chicken coop, a pigsty. It had taken seven months.

They felt they were living apart from the world, but also so close to everything that they could be happy forever.

On Augusto Severo Square, Fefedo was already managing the drug den. He had tried renting a flat for the family, but his parents did not want it. They knew of the illicit trade their son was involved in, and tried everything to get him out of his criminal life. Fefedo would not budge. It was not his fault that they were there.

The only person in the family that Fefedo communicated with was Chico. Behind the backs of his parents, who pretended not to know what was happening, he sent his younger brother the best food, and invited him over to his flat to sleep and shower.

José was increasingly worried about Lúcia's advanced pregnancy. He was scared that she would give birth on the streets. One day, lamenting to a friend, he found out that the mayor Djalma Maranhão had offered some homeless street dwellers a piece of land. The friend told him that only "Big Man" Pedro had chosen to build his home there. The piece of land was large and there was enough space to build a house as big as you wanted it to be. The friend also told him that the "Big Man" Pedro had started raising chickens, goats and sheep. Dona Luíza had planted a large vegetable garden and an orchard. The couple did not have to spend any money on food. The money they made was for medicine, for clothes and for small daily expenses.

José, Lúcia and their children set out early on a Sunday morning. Lúcia could hardly move, she kept holding her belly, and had to stop frequently to catch her breath. José was scared by the dense and inhospitable environment. It would not be easy to live there. Chico was terrified by prospect of being bitten by a snake. He kept quiet as his father told his mother that the house of "Big Man" Pedro and Luíza was deep inside the scrub. Lúcia did not want to go, she was in no state. José told her to wait with Chico, Regina and Neuza. He would go alone. He would build a hut there, an improvised hut, he would build it any way he could. No more sleeping under awnings. The mayor had given away some land. If he built them a small hut now, he could later expand it into a larger house. He started walking into the scrub, wondering if he should bring Lúcia with him. Perhaps she might see and like "Big Man" Pedro's and Luíza's house. She could sense his hesitation, and asked him to wait for her. She and the children would come along if he walked very slowly.

Neuza carried Chico on her back. She knew that her brother was terrified of snakes. The dog walked ahead, scaring off any animals, while the parrot flew low alongside them.

It was a long holiday. The people who usually bought weed and cocaine were away. Marçal Aquino, the drug den's boss, had dipped into the cash to pay for his mother's surgery at a private hospital. The den had no money. Three policemen arrived, expecting their cut, but Fefedo had no cash. Because of the holiday, the men who appeared were different to the ones who usually showed up to collect their bribes.

Policemen only treat criminals well when they can be sure they will make some money off them. One of the them pulled his gun on Fefedo, who was not intimidated and said he wasn't scared of being shot. The other two had to intervene to avoid an escalation. Fefedo said that since he'd been managing the operation, the three policemen who usually picked up the bribes had never left empty-handed. He asked for two days to get them their money, every cent of it. The holiday and the boss' mother's surgery had left him with no cash. Before leaving, the policeman stared sinisterly at Fefedo. Things had changed. A standoff between a policeman and a criminal can only be resolved when one of them kills the other. There was something else: those three policemen were the same ones that had beaten up Fefedo's parents and siblings the day the family arrived in the city and slept on the beach. Perhaps God had sent them back his way.

Two days went by. The following night the policemen went to the drug den to get their bribe money. Fefedo, his face darkened by the strong sun, put the money into the hands of the one who had threatened him. As the man counted the money, Fefedo pulled out a gun and ordered the three policemen into their van. He told the one who was driving to go fast. They arrived at an abandoned lot where Fefedo killed the three of them. Then he calmly went back to the den with the money.

Lúcia was walking into the scrub with great difficulty. She hardly had the strength to worry about the snakes, which José scared off with a large tree branch. She was panting, sweat running down her face, hand on her belly, she regretted having gone, but when she caught the first glimpse of "Big Man" Pedro's and Dona Luíza's house she could not help a wide smile – the smile that always lit up her face whenever she remembered that moment, or told someone about it.

She was reminded of her old home, back in the time when the rains still fell on that corner of the world where she was born and raised. The whole family was surprised and delighted to see the house. They stopped to admire it from a distance. Then they walked towards it, causing the dogs to stir.

The dogs' noise brought Dona Luíza to her window, from where she observed each of the visitors. Her eyes narrowed as she saw the heavily pregnant Lúcia. She ran to meet her, put her hand on Lúcia's forehead to check her temperature, then took her wrist to check her pulse, hardly hearing the rest of the family's greetings. She asked José to carry his wife into the house and put her on a bed. After

Lúcia's water broke, she gathered the instruments she would need for the makeshift birth. She examined Lúcia again, and noted that there was still time for José to clean up his wife.

Pedro prepared some food for Neuza, Regina and Chico and served it on a wooden table at the back of the yard. He told the children that the pain of childbirth was very great. Their mother would scream, but it would all pass soon. Regina knew this already. She had heard her mother's screams when her siblings were born. Only Chico, youngest among the children, had never heard such screams.

Marçal Aquino told Fefedo he had done the right thing. Those policemen were surely going to cause trouble. Why could they not wait one day to get their kickbacks? Fefedo had to put a bullet in them. He had also done the right thing by killing them far away from the den. Someone would have certainly seen Fefedo pulling a gun on the policemen, but no one would dare turn him in. Everyone there liked him, and in that place it was the dealers who called the shots. The police only showed up to take their cut from the den and from other businesses.

The birth was calm. Lúcia did not scream a lot. As she said herself, if giving birth to a second child was easier than the first, then pushing out the fifth one felt very easy indeed.

Chico looked at Severino, determined to protect him throughout his life, to understand him in all situations, to be a friend, to put an arm around him to ward off the troubles of poverty, to defend him from all the evil that people and the sun can inflict on human beings. He would teach his youngest sibling to read, to climb trees, to use a knife and fork, and so many other things he himself did not even know yet. He would help him understand the pains of daily life, understand hunger, avoid thirst, and survive the devouring heat with which the sun punishes the earth, and which later radiates out of the dry earth to make the body ache.

Luíza handed Severino over to José. The man kissed his newborn son's forehead and passed him on to Regina, who repeated the gesture and handed the baby to Neuza. Chico had to sit down before he was able to hold his baby brother in his arms. Only then did the baby stop crying.

Lúcia was both happy and sad because she was also thinking of Fefedo. She felt huge grief in her chest, and she knew the reason. She should be over the moon, because giving birth to a child, even amid great poverty, was a good thing, tempering the darkness of today's real life with the imagined light of the future. But her unease was greater even than the pain of childbirth, it felt like a premonition of death pounding on her soul.

She listened as José spoke to "Big Man" Pedro, who said that moving to that place had been the best thing he had ever done. Their life there was much better. The food came straight from the ground, and from the animals they raised. He had a roof to protect them from the flames that God lit in the sky. He had found a way to store water from the rain, that always seemed to fall.

José could count on "Big Man" Pedro's help to build his own home. He wanted a wattle-and-daub house. If he built it over stones, if he found some good wood, if he packed the mud properly, if he covered it with a thatch of tree leaves, it would be perfect. He could leave his family with Luíza and Pedro while he built his house. Everything was good in that place, but it needed more people. Neighbors, the smiles of wandering children, a friend to talk to at night over a drink of cachaça before bedtime.

Fefedo was surprised when he did not see his family on the square. He worried that something bad had happened, that his brother had been born and they had needed to take shelter somewhere far away. He missed Chico. He waited until the early morning, before his father went to work on the building site, to speak to José.

José hugged Fefedo, and told him that Severino was born in full health. He told him that they now had a place to live. They were staying with a friend who had built his own house overnight and was like a brother. He urged Fefedo to leave the life of crime. Fefedo could help him build their house, then a vegetable garden, an orchard, raise the animals he liked so much. The boy said he would join him one day. He offered José some money so that he could build a brick house, but José refused, with tears in his eyes. Fefedo kissed his father's forehead.

"Leave that life, son."

"It's too late now, dad."

"You should never have gone down that path."

"I wouldn't have gone down that path if we hadn't come to the city. I swear that if the rains start falling again back home I'll return. I wasn't ready for life in the city, or to work like a slave. There should be no rich people."

"But you could get killed anytime."

"The only thing I care about in the world is you."

Fefedo ran his hands over his father's eyes, trying to wipe his tears, and kissed him.

"I won't be a slave of the rich folk in the big city. Pray for rain back home, dad. Maybe God will listen. I have no voice to pray, and I have no clean hands to make the sign of the cross."

José's tears rolled down as he stood in silence while Fefedo walked away down the road, as unchangeable as the past.

Fefedo crossed the road. It was not his usual time to be out and about, as he was always selling drugs at night and waking up at lunchtime. Now just wanted to have a quick breakfast.

He greeted one of his sellers with a nod, went up to the bakery counter, ordered a coffee and a buttered bread. That was when he saw five police cars arriving at the corner. He kept his calm, looked in the opposite direction and noticed more cars approaching.

It was Luíza who chose the place for her new friends to build their home. A flat stretch of land, with a view of the beach and with no rainwater coursing through. Soon Lúcia started calling her *Mãe* Luíza – Mother Luíza. She was the woman who had delivered her child, who had offered the family water, food and shelter, and who was now helping her build the home in which she would live with her children and husband. Only someone with the vocation to become a mother to all who needed her could be so generous.

Slowly they cleared the land, flattened the ground, hoed the earth where they would have an orchard and a vegetable garden. They did it all joyfully. Lúcia, with Severino in her arms, looked around and felt saddened at not being able to enjoy the happiness life was offering her. She was torn between her gladness about the new home and the sorrow caused by her eldest son.

Fefedo drank his coffee calmly. He saw his seller being arrested as he tried to run away. Without letting the nervousness show, he asked for an orange juice. Discreetly he felt for the trigger of the gun tucked into his trousers. He paid his bill, left the bar, looked out for the place with the most policemen and walked towards them. Two black boys happened to be going the same way. He moved with determination, assertive, looking ahead, and smiled to himself when the cops stopped the two black boys. He walked calmly towards the building site where his father worked.

The black boys, who could not prove they were employed, were punched and kicked by the police. They were thrown into a police van despite protesting that they were not criminals, but simply unemployed and looking for work. The more they said the more they were beaten up. The only remedy was to remain silent.

At the building site, Fefedo told his father that he wanted to meet Severino. José looked around the square, tried to read the situation, and asked his son to stay on the building site that day. The boy understood the plan, and agreed. The foreman, who was also worried, did not only allow Fefedo to stay but agreed to pay him a day's wages.

Fefedo got to work with the clothes he was wearing. He was skilled. When they lived on the fazenda, he always helped his father, and was almost as good as José at painting.

When they left the building site, Fefedo chose not to wash himself. He walked out carrying his work tools, his body and his clothes covered in paint. The police had left the area. The radio reported that they had caught the suspects of the three policemen's murders. Using hand signs, Fefedo told his other sellers on the square that he would make himself scarce for a while. From one of the square's benches, Marçal Aquino gave him the thumbs up.

When Lúcia saw her eldest son, she ran towards him carrying Severino. Baleia wagged her tail, the parrot perched on Fefedo's shoulder.

"He looks just like you."

Chico pulled an angry face, saying that Severino actually looked more like him. Everyone laughed. Lúcia introduced Fefedo to "Big Man" Pedro and Mãe Luíza.

Fefedo hardly spoke as they had dinner, but he was brimming with happiness as he saw his family in that place, so lush and full of life. "Big Man" Pedro suggested that he should build his own house there.

When he was asked about his work, Fefedo replied that he had worked on site with his father that day, but did not know whether he might be allowed back the next. His father and mother knew that he was not being completely truthful. After dinner, talking outside in the yard, they spoke openly.

"I don't like the city, I don't like the police, I don't like having a boss, I don't like rich people."

"Son, that's the way of the world, changing anything is a struggle. I'm your mother, and I don't want to see my son in jail or killed by the cops."

"Better to die than to work for the rich. That building dad is painting? He will never be allowed in when it's done."

"I know, but wasn't it the same at the fazenda? Nothing there was really ours. I worked there my whole life and owned none of it."

"Yes, dad, but there at least we had our own little house, we had food on our table, there were no policemen beating poor people up just because they have nowhere to sleep. The rich hate the poor, they just want our labor, our sweat. And we're not even black. It's much worse if you're black."

"But you're not going to change anything going on like that. Better for you to come here. Build your own house, start growing things. Something is telling me that you should not go back to the city center now."

"Okay, mom, I'll stick around here for a few days."

Lúcia hugged Fefedo. José joined in their embrace. Father and mother thought the situation with their son was resolved.

On the square, there were policemen everywhere carrying Fefedo's spoken portrait. It was the owner of the bar who had described the boy at the police station. He usually treated the drug dealers well, he got protection from the gangs, but deep down he hated them all. His son had become addicted to cocaine, had left his wife and young child, and had been roaming the streets, lost in his addiction, until he died. The bar owner had only become friendly with the drug dealers because he had no choice. When he went to the police station to denounce Fefedo, he said he had seen him pull a gun on the policemen, and order them to get into the police van. He also said that he had seen him on Rua Barata many times. That was surely the street where he lived, and his family must live nearby. It was Fefedo's luck that the bar owner did not know José worked at a building site close to the bar.

The police turned Fefedo's apartment upside down. They found nothing other than some clothes. There were no drugs and no

documents to identify him. The police went around the square,
found Marçal Aquino and interrogated him. Marçal Aquino said
that none of his men would ever kill a cop, much less three at once.
He was just working there, doing his business, as he had been doing
for over ten years, and he had always had a good relationship with
the police.

The police officer said that Fefedo must surely be out of his
mind, and that they would not rest until they found him. It was
then that Marçal Aquino suggested increasing the payoff. He said
he would pay the cops twice what he was giving them every week.
He argued that the cops had already arrested the black youths, they
could just charge them and close the case.

It was all in hand, the policeman said. They would charge the
black kids. They would not even be there, he said, were it not for
the bar owner who had grassed on Fefedo. Marçal Aquino looked
over at the bar while the policemen pointed out that its owner was
the only person complaining about sales of drugs in the area. The
policeman himself had been at the station when the owner came in
to rat on Fefedo.

The eldest son walked deeper into the scrubland followed by the
parrot and by Baleia, determined to build his house in a place that
was difficult to reach.

He decided to build his house on a spot from which all the paths
to the property could be easily guarded. José helped Fefedo build it.
With the money he had saved, Fefedo bought what he needed to
furnish it, and he remained there for nearly two months, deliberately staying away from the drug den.

When he finally decided to speak to Marçal Aquino, things got
heated. They argued for close to two hours. Fefedo claimed that
he had seen in the murdered policeman's face the determination
to extract revenge for not getting his payoff. It might not have been
the money, perhaps just the pure hate every cop carries in his heart.

He had seen the evil in the man's eyes. To make amends, Fefedo agreed to return to the den twice more to make enough money to double the cops' payoff. Marçal Aquino also told Fefedo that it was the bar owner who had ratted him out.

"A coffee, please."

The bar owner's eyes narrowed as he looked at Fefedo, who smiled as he savored the prospect of revenge. The man was scared, convinced that the criminal was there to kill him, but Fefedo continued smiling conspicuously, saying he was happy because his favorite team had won the championship in Rio de Janeiro. He supported Flamengo, which had beaten Vasco three-nil. The bar owner blanched when the boy pointed a gun at him, nodding at him to leave the bar quietly.

The man had no choice. They got into a waiting taxi that drove them down to the beach, where they sat side by side at the water's edge.

"I heard you ratted me out to the pigs. No point lying. That's why we're here. I'll kill you and feed you to the fish."

"For the love of God, have mercy, don't do that!"

"I won't kill you on one condition: you go back to the police station, tell them you were wrong. Tell them you'd been drinking. Tell them the ones you really saw getting into the police car with the cops were those black kids. Tell them you only realized this when you saw their photos in the papers."

And so it happened. The police chief found it odd, but he believed the man. That night when the policemen arrived to get their cut, the bar owner went to talk to them, as agreed with Fefedo.

"How could you mistake them, the kids are black, and the other guy is white?"

"I thought he might have been with them, but I'd already had a few drinks."

The policemen believed it, or pretended to believe it, as the police chief had done before. The case was closed.

Marçal Aquino was pleased by Fefedo's quick thinking. He was surprised when Fefedo said, flashing a calm and quick smile, that he would continue selling drugs, but he would no longer sleep in the flat he had rented. He told Marçal Aquino that he had rented another place somewhere else in the city.

With their son returning to his home every day, Lúcia and José felt much more at ease. They were sure that it was just a matter of time before he gave up his life of crime and made peace with the sun, since water was no longer scarce.

Time passed. To Mãe Luíza's and "Big Man" Pedro's delight, Valdir, Oswaldo and Joana also decided to move to the area after hearing José talking with such enthusiasm about his new home. They slowly built their houses, as did the others who had fled the drought in Lagoa Salgada. Soon they had created a small hamlet.

When she went into town, Lúcia sometimes brought back pregnant women who she found living on the streets. She told them they could come to a wonderful place with an excellent midwife, and a shelter for them to recover after giving birth. Some women went along with their husbands; others, abandoned by their babies' fathers, went on their own. At the new settlement they found support and care. Then they often found work as maids. They left their children under the care of Mãe Luíza, who loved them, and who looked after them when they were sick. Many children came into the world at the hands of Mãe Luíza, who also helped many of those new mothers, cowardly abandoned with their babies, to build their huts. And so, the settlement grew.

Sabino liked poetry, he recognized himself in it even before he could read. Whenever he heard someone reciting a verse, or when he listened to music, something inside him pushed him to be a better person, wherever he happened to be. He did not want to be top of the class, or the best at sport, or the most popular with the girls. He wanted to be the best at making people around him happy. Above everything else, he wanted to be a good friend to others. Everything in life was there for his own good, so he liked all things – even if some of those things were not very nice, because after all there was always the possibility of things changing for the better. For him, everything could be transformed. Only nothingness was bad, because it did not have the power to change. He preferred abstract nouns because they meant almost the same for everyone: love is love, full stop. Concrete nouns change, they are different for everyone, they get lost, they break, they are altered, they can vanish – nouns like house, food, health, school.

That was how he felt when he read the Bible. There, in those pages, he found poetry filled with the greatest humanity that any person can aspire to. He did not want to be Christ, he wanted simply, and above all else, to follow the example of Christ's simplicity and love. He learned that the best position people might find themselves in is to be helping others, whether close or distant. So, he left home aged eleven to study at a school run by the Salesian order. He wanted to become a priest. After being ordained, he readied himself to work in poor countries in the Americas, Asia or Africa, anywhere that his congregation was carrying out its mission.

He arrived in Brazil at the age of 34. His destination had been chosen by his superiors. He was to become headmaster at the Salesian school in Natal.

As at home in the new settlement, Fefedo did not even smoke weed. He helped the family with the happy task of carrying water to fill the water barrels, he cleared the scrub to enlarge the vegetable garden and orchard, and helped build other people's huts, which seemed to multiply every day.

The settlement grew so much that it was named Mãe Luíza, in honor of the woman who had delivered the babies of the women who arrived heavily pregnant, and who cared for them until they could carry on with their lives. On Sundays she cooked and invited people over for lunch. But time passed, and she was starting to feel tired. She was not yet aware that she was sick, but she lacked the motivation she had shown since the day she moved there.

Fefedo continued dealing drugs. To avoid getting into further trouble in the place where he started his life of crime, he started selling in another part of the city. There he ran into Lelé, and was not too pleased about it. Lelé also lived in Mãe Luíza. Nobody there knew what either of them did for a living. He told Fefedo that he wanted to carry on with his life in Mãe Luíza without anyone finding out. He had known for some time about Fefedo, but had said nothing to keep things quiet. Fefedo soon adopted Lelé's approach to living in their new community. Mãe Luíza had to be their refuge, a place of rest, a place for family life, a place where they could fall asleep with both eyes closed, without needing to keep one of them on the police while the other was on their dreams. They needed to protect their families, have a place that would not attract anyone's attention. Fefedo felt the determination in Lelé's expression and the assurance in his words. He had found a new friend, who also became his small-scale dealer, or *vapor*.

But the part of the city where he was working now was less safe than where he was selling before. It was close to Passo da Pátria, where the police often showed up looking for criminals on the run and for stolen goods. The other problem was the huge foot traffic around the drug den. Buyers and more buyers, at all hours of the day. A lot of cash changed hands. So, cops were always after the money. But the worst problem was the rival drug gang, intent on taking over that profitable sales point.

Speaking to Lelé and Fefedo, Marçal Aquino confessed his worry that traffickers from another part of the city might try to take over his sales point because of its high turnover. In Rio de Janeiro there was warfare between rival gangs over sales points. Marçal had grown up in Natal, people on the street knew and respected him, but even so he knew he had to be careful because rivals might have an eye on his profits.

On Praça Augusto Severo, the square that was Marçal Aquino's turf, the volume of sales was lower, buyers were mostly university students, theatre types and musicians who just wanted to get their kicks smoking weed, talking about art and science and culture. The demand for cocaine was not very high, but the return was good because it was expensive. Only the rich bought it, although nobody knew who they were. The rich users never went to the drug den themselves, they sent others to get the stuff for them.

Business was good because the den had been going for awhile. Marçal Aquino had started when he was a boy, running errands for the traffickers and buying them things at the bakery, the pharmacy or the market. He became a lookout before becoming a *vapor*. As time passed, his employers got killed off one at a time, or went to jail for refusing to hand over half of their profits to the police. Marçal Aquino preferred to negotiate. He believed that it was better for crooks like him to reach agreements with the police, not pick fights with them. He made a tidy sum, but did not let on with the police, and so he managed to carry on. He expanded his business when a middle-class dope user told him that there were many people near Praça Augusto Severo who wanted to buy drugs but were afraid of going to where he was selling them. Marçal said he would send a dealer with some thirty weed bags every Friday. That was how the drug den started. The place was lively but relatively safe, because the police did not show up firing shots and killing innocent passers-by. It was not the kind of poor man's place that the police hated.

In Mãe Luíza, life continued happily for Chico, who liked carrying Severino on his shoulders and walking out into the wooded areas. They spent the day playing with other children, young and old. They killed snakes, hunted birds, played all sorts of children's games.

Mãe Luíza and "Big Man" Pedro were beginning to worry about the number of people moving to their settlement. This included the families of pregnant women whose babies Mãe Luíza delivered, always with great love and affection. But besides lacking running water, the place also lacked sewage and a doctor's practice and a school. In some ways the Mãe Luíza settlement was a sort of paradise, but there was no government help. Hunger afflicted people's bodies. Famished and scrawny mothers, all skin and bones, carried their malnourished children as they begged for money at traffic lights on Salgado Filho or Prudente de Morais avenues. Rich people were now beginning to build their own houses in the vicinity of the Mãe Luíza settlement, and they did not want all those wretched survivors of the drought at their doorstep. The history of the Mãe Luíza community was marked by its residents' struggle to remain on their own land.

Chico had not yet understood that money does not bring happiness, but he knew that its absence brings hunger, misery, malnourishment, disease, and lack of schooling. All those things come together to cause constant pain, which turns into anger, then hatred, and then becomes a gunshot.

Fefedo and Lelé told the policemen they would get a weekly cut of three thousand cruzeiros. They were cautious and insisted on having an agreed system. They would not be handing out money to all the patrol cars showing up at all times of day. The cops could sort the payments out among themselves. They also had to let the dealers know the days and times when they would show up to collect their bribes. No coming in brandishing guns, because no one there was going to be shooting at them. Also, no harassing the users that loitered around the drug den.

Marçal Aquino, who controlled the area, would not allow any sort of misbehavior in the neighborhood or its surroundings. He guaranteed that on their patch there would be no criminality.

The policemen were surprised by the suggestion, but they agreed to the deal when they heard that Fefedo was offering them twice as much as they had been getting. As they were leaving, Fefedo said out loud:

"Remember that we are *malandros*. And *malandros* don't fight, they reach agreements. Here, on my patch, you won't hear a single shot."

The policemen nodded. Every place should be managed like that, they said. If things were always kept quiet like that, people everywhere would sleep better.

With no constant policing, the number of users grew. The patch was quiet. Fefedo and Lelé were raking in more money. The cops were happy. Marçal Aquino was delighted.

But all was not well in Mãe Luíza. News of the place was spreading. More people arrived every day. Now there were even some speculators marking out large plots of land, fencing them up, building small huts in some of the best remaining places and then selling them on, even if only for a small profit.

Lelé and Fefedo wanted to stay out of it, letting things happen. If they spoke up, everyone would know who they were and the peace and quiet they enjoyed would be over. Better to keep quiet despite the settlement's disorderly expansion, the badly built wooden shacks, the pools of mud that formed on the busier lanes.

They stopped at a local bar one day for a drink and a snack. They were surprised to see three armed boys shouting that they had cocaine and weed to sell. The three kids bought drugs somewhere far away and then re-sold it with a fifty percent markup. They had started out stealing food because of the hunger they experienced during the drought, back home in the interior. They went into markets and stuffed food into their clothes, but more often than not they were caught and beaten up by the security guards who handed them over to the police. They would spend some time locked up, but would soon be released because they were not considered dangerous. Until one of them managed to get his hands on a gun.

Things were not going well at Luíza's house, either. She had even stopped delivering other people's babies after she got cancer and lost her desire to take care of others, alongside her appetite and her sex drive. She did not want "Big Man" Pedro to abandon her, but she knew it might happen because he still felt the stirrings of desire and, despite her ongoing reluctance, was constantly propositioning her. In the end she agreed to him taking a mistress. This was a surprise to all those who held the couple in such high esteem.

Lúcia was particularly saddened, and stayed in bed, wondering if José might do the same to her. No, her husband was not a saint, he was far from perfect, but she would not make the same mistake.

Meanwhile, Fefedo continued his life of crime. He was still enraged at having been forced to leave his ancestral home. He blamed the sun. But now he lived somewhere else, he could find an honest job, go to night school, then university, and help improve his and his family's circumstances.

Lúcia was well-informed, she read the news in the newspapers used to wrap the food that José brought home. She liked to know about politics and the economy, and about what was happening in the city. She understood that the Mãe Luíza settlement was now a notorious neighborhood, complete with its own criminals who were nothing more than the product of a society that, since the time of Brazil's colonization, had been unfair to black people, to immigrants fleeing the droughts, and to native Brazilians. Newspapers published unfavorable headlines about the neighborhood but never explained why the bad things happened. Lúcia knew that wealthy Brazilians looked favorably on the United States and on some European countries, former slave-trading nations that now claimed to be goodies, but in reality took part in the economic policies that cause hunger, unemployment and misery on poorer continents.

She felt relief and subdued happiness for Regina and Neuza who were now working as maids, with no contract, for some of the city's rich ladies. They took care of everything in these rich ladies' houses, with no agreed clocking-out time. They slept in that modern version of the slave quarters that people call the maids' rooms, less than one meter across, barely able to stretch out their legs on the rickety beds put in by their employers. But she was happy to know that the girls were living far away from the Mãe Luíza neighborhood where the police now showed up firing shots into the air, frisking everyone, beating people up, even despite being there to claim the paltry bribes that the local *vapores* were able to offer them. Her biggest concern was Chico, who still liked going out with Severino in his arms and walking through what remained of the wooded area near the neighborhood to climb trees and pick fruit. He had made friends, and among them were some of the kids who stole because they had no food at home, because they had no clothes to wear, the kids who stole out of necessity. Lúcia was sad, she was depressed even though she did not know what depression meant. She wanted to end it all, but did not kill herself due to the love she felt for her children and her will to see Fefedo walk a straight path.

The atmosphere became tense in the drug den with the arrival of three dealers who had blown in from somewhere else. They had their eyes on the profits that Fefedo was bringing in. They came in wanting to know where Fefedo was getting his weed and coke, because what they were selling was bad quality. Lelé was already standing close to the guns, but stood down when Fefedo signaled that it was all okay and, without showing any concern, explained to the newcomers that his product was indeed better because he had a big market, and the wholesaler knew that.

"And who is your wholesaler?"

"I don't know who the big boss is, and never will. He doesn't even know we exist. I only speak to his minion, who comes here to sell the stuff."

"Got it. I also have my minions working for me. I don't want to be the one fronting things. I want to be like one of those rich guys that nobody knows."

Fefedo thought it was funny, but when the kid pointed out that not even Fefedo had recognized him, Fefedo looked more closely and remembered having seem him around Mãe Luíza. He was always alone, playing with some child. The kid said that Mãe Luíza would be a good place to sell, because if the cops showed up, there were many places to run to. He said he would not be selling it himself, he'd ask someone else to do the work for him, like those rich people.

Fefedo wanted no trouble in the place that had become his refuge, but said that he could introduce the kid to Marçal Aquino. He was sure that Marçal Aquino might agree to opening up another sales point. The kid laughed and said that he had already spoken to Marçal. And Marçal had already agreed to the proposal, but was not sure if Fefedo would like it. Fefedo laughed.

"What's your name?"

"Lourenço. These guys here are Mário and Aderaldo."

The others approached to shake hands with Fefedo. Lelé moved away from the guns to greet their new friends.

The Mãe Luíza neighborhood was now home to hundreds of malnourished and underpaid workers, the unemployed, beggars, maids, children with no school, no health care and no dental care. It was a snapshot of Brazil: open sewers, refuse on the streets, people dying of hunger, the sick with no access to medicine, rats everywhere and babies dying of diarrhea. On top of everything there was a drug den, managed in a very orderly way and attracting the youth who saw in it the chance to make easy money. The sales point expanded and now had many boys taking turns at selling the product.

Lourenço, Mário and Aderaldo would not allow any speculation with property. They came down hard on Florisvaldo, who took other people's land and sold it off. He was a big man who carried a gun, and pushed people off their own properties. One day he woke up a family that had sunk all its savings into buying a little house in the middle of the scrub. Mother, father and two children had finally realized the cherished dream of owning their own house. They had arrived shortly after Lúcia, who had helped them choose the plot of land where they would build their home. The plot of land had increased in value because it was now at the bottom corner of Mãe Luíza's main road.

Florisvaldo was a sort of real estate broker. As the community grew, he fenced off many plots of land and sold them to whoever wanted to buy. That particular time, a businessman wanted a place to open a corner shop, and the family's house would be the perfect place. Florisvaldo asked for a high price, which the man was willing to pay. Not knowing that the neighborhood now had a local drug boss who set the rules, Florisvaldo knocked down the family's door, and told them to collect their documents and whatever clothes they could carry, because the property was now his. Florisvaldo did not expect the family to complain to Lourenço, Mário and Aderaldo. The three of them caught up with Florisvaldo. Besides giving him a good beating, they shot him in the foot and expelled him from Mãe Luíza.

The good news arrived that the municipality had decided to build a school. The bad news was that the school relied on some very retrograde methods of teaching. Teachers still used spanking paddles to punish students, who were also made to kneel on corn kernels. On top of that, there were not enough places for all the students in Mãe Luíza to enroll.

Another new arrival was Father João Perestrello, who bought a hut and founded a community center. The site supported children's education, and helped residents organize to demand improvements for the Mãe Luíza neighborhood from the municipal and state governments. Then came Father Aloysio, who helped bolster the community center. A nursery school was set up, allowing the youngest children to begin their education. Not much importance was given to the religious side of things. Whoever wanted to pray the Our Father or Hail Mary could do so, but those who did not would not be excluded.

Adelaide wasted no time. When she saw all those malnourished girls, begging for money on the beach, she spoke to Lourenço, Mário and Aderaldo. She asked them to buy a house that was deep inside the scrub, out of the way, in the section they called Ribiera, and open a little club with multiple rooms and a good kitchen. She would transform those wretched but pretty girls into prostitutes, and they would rake the money in. She added that the girls would have to be well remunerated. Otherwise, they would be having sex through gritted teeth, and everyone knows that a whore performing as an obligation is like cold coffee. Nobody likes it.

And so it was. In less than five months the brothel was up and running, the girls were well treated, well fed, and having sex all day long with brutes. The men would buy weed and go straight to the club, where they drank, ate and then demanded sex with the girls. The policemen were given preferential treatment.

No one had seen Fefedo cry since he was seven years old. Whenever something bad happened, his eyes narrowed, his face grew serious, anticipation of revenge growing in his soul. But that day, when he found everyone standing in the garden, he broke down in the deepest sobs. Chico and Severino had gone to play in the woods followed by Baleia. When they were on their way, some policemen arrived firing shots all over the place. There had been a robbery in the Tirol neighborhood, and they needed to kill someone to prove that they had caught the robbers, who had subsequently died in an exchange of fire. One of the shots got Baleia square in the head. The parrot, which had witnessed everything, dropped dead, killed by his grief.

When he saw his dead pets laid out over a blanket, Fefedo wept inconsolably. José did not have the strength to lift his son into his arms. Lúcia hugged the boy, who put his head on his mother's shoulder.

Fefedo was not one of those people who love animals more than people, but he saw in Baleia and the parrot the beauty of his childhood without the sadness that now weighed over his life. His pets reminded him of the fields through which he had run with an open smile, chasing after nothing. And what was that nothing? The plants, the birds singing under the awnings, the water in the stream that he crossed in bare feet, the fruit in the trees and all the things that took him back to his boyhood. He never expected the happiness to end like that, with a shot from a trigger-happy policeman who enjoyed killing the poor and everything that comes with them, including their pets.

He dug two small graves in front of his hut, and he buried the two animals himself. He went home and, on his knees, prayed to Our Lady of Aparecida and to St. Joseph. After praying he took the images and gave them to his mother, so that she might pray for him and for their family the rest of the day. He was sure that his own prayers would not be heard. He prayed for the sake of praying. That day he prayed for his past, and for the souls of his pets, because he had nothing to pray for in the present. His animals belonged to a time when he lived in peace. If his family had stayed at home, his dog would not have taken a shot. Baleia would die a natural death, as it should always be.

Fefedo decided he would no longer work as Marçal Aquino's street
seller. The death of his pets filled him with rage. How can anyone
shoot a defenseless animal? He remembered the day the cops beat
his parents, and then he remembered the three wretched cops dying
at his hands. He was going to change his life, he would make more
money and take his family to where the rich people lived. He would
do what Marçal Aquino did and, after a while, he would be like the
rich boss, the one that never showed his face, the one that no one
knew but who owned everything.

That day he made his way to the sales point, gave Lelé his instruc-
tions and then left. When he got back to Mãe Luíza, he stopped at
a bar close to the drug den and gruffly ordered a beer. When Lourenço, Mário and Aderaldo came up to him he said he wanted half
of the profits because the den only existed thanks to him. Fefedo's
stern look and tone of voice made the dealers agree without hesitation. Fefedo was pleased to see their positive response. When there
was no one else looking to buy weed they all went to the *forró* dance
at Seu Mané's place, where they drank more and danced until the
late hours. Later, Fefedo went to the brothel, where he had sex with
three women and slept until noon.

When he left the brothel, he could not understand why there was
such a large crowd walking towards the beach. Only when he came
close did he see "Big Man" Pedro crying and carrying Mãe Luíza's
coffin with José, Lúcia, Regina and Neuza. Mãe Luíza had died
while seated on a bench with Chico and Severino feeding corn to
the chickens.

The coffin was put onto the hearse. Everyone else walked to
the main road to get on the old bus that would take them to the
cemetery.

Mãe Luíza was deserted when Fefedo arrived at the den where
Lourenço, Mário and Aderaldo watched the dealers selling pot.
With his deadpan expression, Fefedo asked Aderaldo to go find

50 wraps of cocaine with Lelé, at the drug den where he used to sell, and to say that he would settle the payments later.

Whenever someone came to buy weed, Fefedo would ask the three partners whether that customer was a serious user. He wanted to know everything about the users – were they unemployed, were they stealing, were they drinking? He gave them cocaine for free, saying it was better than weed, it did not have a recognizable smell, it gave a buzz that lasted for hours and hours, it was a rich person's drug, and if the police showed up while they were using it it was a lot easier to dispose of – all they needed was to blow it away to avoid getting caught. For a week, he handed out the cocaine to those he thought most likely to get hooked.

Time passed and soon the den was selling more cocaine than weed. Lourenço, Mário and Aderaldo started wearing expensive clothes, bought themselves cars, expanded their homes and went out with women who, like them, enjoyed luxuries and wealth.

One Sunday, Fefedo arrived at his parents' house. It had been awhile since he had seen them. They all had stern expressions because they knew about his work in the neighborhood. As always, he asked his parents for their blessing, but they did not say a word. Only Severino greeted him. Not even Chico, his favorite, said anything. He was old enough to understand, and he saw how the family suffered because of his eldest brother's line of work. It was easy to blame the sun and the drought; it was harder to make an honest living, to study and to find work that was honorable.

All of a sudden Lúcia started talking about her son's unlawful life. About how she suffered because of it, about the sleepless nights, filled with worries. Fefedo did not respond, he kept his head down like a child being told off. Lúcia was increasingly upset, her voice becoming louder. Pleading for calm, José looked at Fefedo and said that the boy would surely be able to leave that life behind. Fefedo remained silent. He only raised his eyes when his mother had a heart attack and died.

He stepped forward to help her, but Chico stood in his way saying out loud that she no longer needed help.

"When you could do something for her, you didn't. Now she no longer needs you."

Chico told his brother to leave. Fefedo walked away slowly, listening to the cries of pain of a family that had only just lost the woman who had taken them in, and now lost its mother in such a painful way.

That was not the end of the misfortunes. During the burial, when the undertakers started shoveling dirt onto Lúcia's coffin, José started trembling, bleeding from his mouth, and fell dead into the open grave of the woman he had loved his entire life.

It was Chico who came up with the idea of finding another coffin and burying husband and wife together, so they could spend their eternity holding hands, their hearts together forever even after they had stopped beating.

"Big Man" Pedro was next to go. After Mãe Luíza's death, and despite his young mistress's attentions, he became a shadow of his former self. He stopped eating, he hardly drank any water, and he died sitting on the sandy beach and looking out at the sea, imagining he was watching Luíza swimming in the waves. He left with a smile on his face.

His funeral was also a big affair. Almost all residents of the Mãe Luíza neighborhood showed up for the burial, as they had for his wife's. There were prayers and sobs all through the neighborhood's lanes. The people who had fled the drought felt orphaned. The neighborhood was like a glass of water quenching their thirst – and now it had become a place with no father or mother.

From that moment, the place felt like it had no one to lead it – in fact it never had. What it did have now was someone to protect it.

Now Mãe Luíza's boss was Fefedo, who managed the den, who sold cocaine and weed to residents and to outsiders. The business grew every day. Fefedo was in charge, everything hinged on his humor, on the power of his rage, on his rancor, on his hatred of the sun.

With the deaths of Mãe Luíza, "Big Man" Pedro, Lúcia and José, the community lost its backbone. It became a jumble of poor people living together, hungry, with no father or mother, with the pain caused by a variety of diseases, with no one to hear their cries for help and now, without Mãe Luíza to pray for their poverty-blighted bodies. It felt as if the community had lost its roots, the advice from its elders, the voices of experience, and a predisposition to human goodness.

Oswaldo and Joana also died. After their deaths, their children went to São Paulo on the back of a flatbed truck and now they live in Capão Redondo under the control of the criminal gang known as the Primeiro Comando da Capital. They found a little house, which they have been expanding, and they remain there. They aged quickly amid the overcrowded buses, the grueling work, the poor nutrition and the lack of appropriate healthcare.

Brazil is a wretched country of wretched people who take strength from the misery of others. An elite that, because it is white, believes itself to be superior. Nor is Europe any better: it hates blacks, native populations, and the poor. The misery started with colonization, with slavery, with the massacres of natives on which the European and North American economies were built. Everybody knows about the desolation that this elite has wrought across the world, profiting from our misery to this day, alongside rich Brazilians and their descendants who resist the social inclusion of the rest of the population. Fortunately, around the world there are people who show solidarity, people who wish for fairer income distribution. People who seek social and racial equality, and are prepared to fight for it. That is why men and women of Europe and

Brazil can also be brothers and sisters in the construction of a new and better world.

The community grew. People were still arriving from the interior, fleeing droughts. There were more homeless people buying pieces of land from speculators, now protected by Fefedo, who got a percentage of the profits for all property sales.

Chico and Severino grew under the care of Regina and Neuza. Whenever they ran into Fefedo, they crossed the road and pretended not to see him. Chico was the best student at the school despite the bad teachers and stale school lunches. He was determined to do well. He went to Father Perestrello's and Father Aloysio's community center, and spent his afternoons there after school. His interest in the books brought in by the priests, in the stories they told, in the four mathematical operations, in the history of Brazil, was like food for his soul, and drove him forward. He did not dwell on the sadness of the desolate people around him, or, if he did, he saw the possibility of change. Even though he could not predict the future, the hope that lit up his soul was stronger than everything.

Neuza and Regina struggled on, cleaning the houses of employers who paid them less than the minimum wage, with no contract, no Christmas bonus, no holidays, no downtime. They left their employers' houses after lunchtime on Sundays, having cleaned the kitchens, and came back at seven in the morning on Mondays. Sometimes, when guests arrived, the Sunday lunch went on until past five in the afternoon.

They were reassured by the fact that Chico took good care of Severino, and did not spend the whole day loitering on the streets, like all the other boys who grew up with him and who were now thieving and hanging around the drug den, hoping to become *vapores* and running errands for the bosses.

The drug bosses from the city's North Zone – Tutuca, Sérgio and Luiz – went to the Mãe Luíza drug den to see how the business was being run. They had heard that more drugs were sold in Mãe Luíza than anywhere else in the region. They did not arrive together, to avoid drawing attention to themselves. They arrived by foot, shoeless and shirtless. They watched closely and confirmed that the place was, indeed, a pot of gold. So much so that, without anyone else knowing about it, Fefedo had bought two little flats on the Ladeira Sobe e Desce. He stayed at one of them when he finished work. Truth be told, he did not work much – he simply showed up at the den to drop off drugs and pick up cash. The agreement with the police had been good for both sides. The police just expected there to be no robberies in the area, especially in the rich houses around Mãe Luíza, but selling drugs was fine – as long as they got a cut. The police insisted that there be no other newsworthy criminal activity. If drug gangs wanted to kill someone, then let them bury the bodies. No serving up stories for the press, no drawing attention to the place.

Tutuca, Sérgio and Luiz bought some cheap shacks at strategic points in the neighborhood. They wanted to observe the police's comings and goings, and the foot traffic around the drug den. They never walked around together. They did not want to alert anyone to the fact that they were working together, or that they intended to kill all the local dealers – Lourenço, Mário, Aderaldo and Fefedo – at once. It would not be easy. Not only were they armed, but the den's manager, the den's guards and even the *vapores* carried 32- or 38-caliber revolvers.

Tutuca, Sérgio and Luiz realized that it would be impossible for them to get everyone at the same time. There was always one person missing, sometimes more than one. The boss, Fefedo, was hardly ever there. They tried to establish the days and times when he showed up, but sometimes he spent weeks, even months, without appearing. Aderaldo, Lourenço and Mário sometimes went to their boss' apartment and smoked weed. They brought along

women they had seduced the night before by pretending to be good
boys. Tutuca, Sérgio and Luiz did not know how to pull off an
effective hit.

Marçal Aquino was ever closer to Fefedo, and enjoyed the friendship. He liked thinking that the man who had started off working
for him had done well and now made enough money to buy two
flats, even if they were in a poor area, and if he was clever, he might
buy another two and then live comfortably off the rent money without having to work for a rich employer.

Lelé was also laughing all the way to the bank. As the drug den's
only general manager, he made money hand over fist. He bought a
simple house, outside of Mãe Luíza. There he took his family, who
did not know how he made a living. He told them he worked as a
supermarket guard, with no fixed contract so that he could make
more money. He expected to stay in the drug business for a little
longer, until he could buy two or three more houses like his own
and live off the rent.

Lelé was clever. He treated people well, he offered credit, he was
always smiling, so the money came in more easily, with no need
to resort to violence. At home, Lelé's father had often said that a
human being's greatest achievement is to make another person happy. Lelé put that into practice at work. He was already recruiting an
old childhood friend to replace him at the den. He wanted to leave
the business without getting caught, without killing anyone, without stealing from anyone.

Tutuca, Sérgio and Luiz did not know what to do. In their favela
there was no one prepared to help them take over Mãe Luíza. Even
the most downtrodden, the ones who felt pangs of hunger every day,
preferred to rob in markets, shops and bakeries than to enter an
unknown place and exchange shots with unknown gang members.
One solution was to groom the local petty criminals, befriend them,
and turn them against the drug den's managers. Another was to

enroll the *vapores*, whose takings were paltry by comparison to the den's bosses.

Over time they got to know people, made friends with them, identified the community's more malicious youth and talked trash about the drug bosses. They even approached poorer and more ambitious *vapores*. They told them that the distribution of profits, with the *vapores* making close to nothing, was unfair. They tried to get close to Aderaldo, Lourenço and Mário, but realized that they were very loyal to their boss.

The idea was to kill the three of them, wait for Fefedo to show up and put a bullet into him as well. They loitered around the den, doing little favors for the *vapores* who took six-hour shifts every day. That first week they identified the date when Fefedo would come around to collect the earnings, they noted the day and the time when the police would drop by to collect their cut, and they made plans for the following Monday morning.

Tutuca was at one street corner, Luiz at another. Sérgio approached Aderaldo to buy a spliff, and as soon as Aderaldo turned around Sérgio put two bullets into this head. Before Lourenço and Mário could respond, Luiz and Sérgio opened fire on them. Some of the *vapores* coming in for the day's second shift also died when they returned fire, but Mauro, Eduardo and Tatal, who were still on the job, raised their hands in the air and pledged their loyalty to the invaders.

The den had new owners.

Like Lelé and Marçal Aquino, Fefedo learned about his associates' deaths from the newspaper. He was saddened, of course, though not hugely. He said that the sun had dried up his tears, he had not even been able to cry for his mother's death, much less his father's. He would cry for no one. For him, the sun was not only the star that burned bright and caused the droughts. The sun was also those rich people who caused poverty. In the big city, those rich people were easier to spot.

Luckily, everyone dies in the end. And once he was in hell, Fefedo would cause all sorts of misery to those rich people who had lived so well off the backs of the poor. He would be the devil's partner. Fefedo went back to working with Lelé on Fridays as if nothing had happened. He was going to make enough money to buy another apartment, rent it out and retire. The only thing he missed from Mãe Luíza were the girls from the brothel and Mané's *forró* dances. When he thought about his family, he felt the rage that had grown with every step he took since they left their old home. Back there, he had hardly noticed the difference between the rich and the poor. Back there, he would die of thirst, but he would die a happy man. Even Chico, his favorite, had said goodbye to the remains of their ancestors like it meant nothing, the family all claiming that they would die of thirst if they stayed. Better to die there than to sleep on the streets, to eat leftover food, be beaten up by the police on the beach, work as maids like Regina and Neuza, live deep in the scrubland in Mãe Luíza with no basic sanitation, no decent schools, no healthcare, none of the things rich people had more than enough of. He felt rage towards the world and whoever created the world. He wanted to retire and grow old with lots of money so he could go to a private doctor when he was ill, eat whatever he wanted to when he was hungry. He did not want to be rich, no. He only wanted dignity.

Mãe Luíza was cut off by bad weather for almost a month. The police tried, with no success, to find out what was happening. They believed Fefedo had died too, they did not know who was behind the killings, who the new owners of the den were, whether a gang had moved in from another favela. They realized that everything had changed when, as they patrolled Mãe Luíza, trying to find out what had really gone down, they were met with a shower of warning shots that made them run down the lanes. One policeman got a bullet in his shoulder.

Mãe Luíza had changed. Tutuca, Sérgio and Luiz unleashed their hatred on those modern-day exploiters, that class of wretches that protected the rich and massacred the poor. There was no way they would give the police any money at all, because it was the police that had taken their father's life in their own favela. That's right: they were brothers. As children, around six o'clock every evening, they waited for their father to come back from work bearing some sweet or cake that he had bought on credit from a local baker. The father, strong and sturdy, carried all three in his arms and filled them with kisses, giving them all the love in the world. At home he checked their notebooks, helped with their homework, showered, waited for their mother to serve them dinner before, together with her, they sang nursery songs until the boys fell asleep.

One Friday, a payday, their father was coming home with the shopping when the police ordered him to stop and raise his hands. The father did what the police ordered, but he was shot many times anyway. The boys saw one of the policemen frisking the body and taking the father's weekly wages. Sadness became a shadow in those boy's lives. They never again laughed. Things became worse after their mother took to bed and never again drank water, or ate food, or did anything else. She only left her house again to be buried.

The boys survived by begging for money at traffic lights, doing odd jobs in exchange for a pittance, eating leftover scraps. They never went back to school. They were evicted from the family's house for not paying the rent. They slept on the street and felt hunger.

Mauro, Eduardo and Tatal, who were Fefedo's *vapores*, had raised their hands and pledged loyalty to the new bosses to avoid being killed. Having survived, they talked among themselves and decided that they would kill the three brothers as soon as they had the chance.

With the Mãe Luíza den now under control, Luiz went back to his favela, told others what was happening, and took another ten boys back with him to be trained by the *vapores*. It was their moment of glory. Everything was going well. The brothers would be rich.

Mauro, Tatal and Eduardo, the *vapores*, were training recruits for their squad. Assisted by Fefedo and Lelé, they managed to get guns from Marçal Aquino.

Mãe Luíza was now bristling with guns. No more bribes for the police, no more respect for the residents, nothing to stop the shoot-outs, nothing that would not end in a storm of violence.

The first attack by Mauro, Tatal and Eduardo's squad happened early on a Monday night. Luiz, Sérgio and Tutuca thought every-thing was quiet, and that the former *vapores* were on their side but laying low to stay out of trouble.

In truth, the *vapores* were plotting to kill their new bosses, and by doing so remove from their community those who did not belong there. They took positions to be able to shoot their three enemies down.

Tutuca, Luiz and Sérgio were in good spirits. The den was doing well at the start of the week, meaning that the weekend would be profitable. They were snorting cocaine and smoking weed when a bullet from Tatal's gun blew up Tutuca's head. Other shots killed Sérgio and Luiz. The shooting increased. Residents sought safety, no one knew where the bullets were coming from. Bullets were fly-ing everywhere.

Mauro took a bullet. He rolled on the floor in pain.

By coincidence, the policemen were coming into the neighbor-hood when the shooting started. They were trying to find Fefedo and collect their money, and did not understand what all the gun-shots were about. They remained near the entrance to Mãe Luíza until the tumult was over.

When the shooting ended, five policemen entered Mãe Luíza furtively, and walked past the bodies strewn on the ground. They had no idea what had happened. It was obvious to them that this was a war over control of the drug traffic, but they did not know who was trying to take over, or who was in charge of the invading gang. They stopped at a lookout point from which they could see much of the area.

The policemen moved through the lanes and alleys, bent low and trying not to make any noise. The body count of teenagers killed in the shoot-out only increased as they went along.

Mauro did not have the strength to move. Eduardo and Tatal were going to carry him away when they saw the policemen approaching. The boys mistook them for their enemies and opened fire on them. The police returned fire, and the two boys had to leave behind their associate, who took a fatal shot to the head. The police recognized Mauro, and they figured out these were Fefedo's *vapores*. They called out to Tatal and Eduardo, who approached with their arms held up in the air. The policemen lowered their weapons and ordered the two youths to come close. They wanted to understand what was happening. Eduardo wanted to assist Mauro, but the policeman confirmed that he was already dead. Tatal started telling the policemen what was happening, not noticing that three members of the enemy squad were hiding in a place from which they could easily take a shot.

They communicated with signs, and then opened fire. They were not interested in the policemen, and instead targeted the heads of Tatal and Eduardo, who died almost simultaneously.

The cops rushed out, thinking that there were many more bandits hidden nearby. And there were. The shoot-out began once again. No one knew who was a friend and who was a foe, and the shots continued until the break of day.

Events in Mãe Luíza were the most talked about subject in local newspapers and across the city. The police did not enter the community; they remained at the entrances checking who entered and who left, waiting for the criminals' ammunition to run out before moving in, capturing the invaders and getting Fefedo's gang back on the streets and selling drugs again.

What the policemen were not expecting was for Chico Velho, one of the place's oldest residents, to pass guns and ammunition to both gangs. Chico Velho knew who was who, where the gang members met and when to find them. He was an old Navy corporal, and getting hold of guns and ammo was a walk in the park for him.

The war was no longer just about drug sales. Many deaths needed to be avenged. The interlopers had recruited many foot soldiers from Mãe Luíza into their gang. Fefedo's gang also had many more new recruits. The fighting was constant, and everyone got used to it. That was how it was across the whole country; the poor killing each other for money, for a better life.

Caught in the crossfire of the conflict was a population of exploited residents, living in poverty, with no choice but to get used to the daily violence caused by youths who, from the moment of their birth, were marginalized by life. There were moments of truce. For instance, when one of the gangs lost its main leaders, and the remaining members escaped into the streets of the big city, or went to live in another favela, or even got on a flatbed truck bound for the south-west in search of a better life they would never find. They would simply end up moving into even more violent favelas in Rio de Janeiro or São Paulo.

Lelé got to know Marçal Aquino and they became close friends. They stopped selling drugs on the streets. They became wholesale suppliers, and did not even have to carry the drugs to the drug dens. They became rich and travelled to the United States together, each with his own family. They both bought their own car dealership and left drug trafficking forever.

Fefedo stopped selling drugs, bought another apartment, found a job as a porter and lived in the building he worked in. He began a relationship with a woman he met while shopping at the market.

He had offered to carry her bags all the way to the bus stop. They got married and had two children. With the rent money from his apartments, plus his porter's salary, he was able to send them to a private school and provide good quality health care. He lived happily ever after.

Regina and Neuza left Mãe Luíza with Severino and Chico on a flatbed truck bound for Rio de Janeiro. They went to live on Mangueira hill. With the money they had made, the sisters were able to buy a small breeze-block house high on the hill. Severino went to school in the favela's own school, and there he completed high school. He wanted to follow in the footsteps of Chico, who had started working as a gas station attendant, finished high school and then signed up to study at the Federal University of Rio de Janeiro's literature department. He became a teacher and worked in public and private schools. He got his family off Mangueira hill, and moved them to Santa Teresa.

The Mãe Luíza community deteriorated over time, which – like all of life's moments of happiness – flew by. What was once bad became worse. If ten gang members died, twenty new ones appeared. The population grew, hunger was rampant, poverty spread everywhere, children died of the most varied diseases because of the lack of basic medical care, or food. Or because their families had been devastated by misery.

Whenever the gangs broke their deal with the police, the cops arrived shooting right and left. Many years passed like that, and poverty made the tumor of violence grow.

It was a sunny morning. The sort of sunny brightness that shatters the night and blows it away, summoning a dawn filled with colors that words cannot describe.

While the sparrows and hummingbirds, with their glinting feathers, filled the morning with their voices, he came out from behind the clouds he created, pretending to be emerging from the sea.

He streamed in through the slats of window blinds, he warmed the bodies of people on their verandas, on the streets, in their gardens, awakening lovers who slept in each other's arms amid promises of love.

We only see what is illuminated. Nothing can flower, thrive, or grow old without the light of the sun.

No color, no flower, no love can be transformed into the art that makes humans better if the sun does not give us the gift of time, which is the father of all creation.

Sun, the master of that future that Mãe Luíza and "Big Man" Pedro once dreamed for their community.

The sun is the star that chose to live closer to humanity. Without its fire, water cannot be transformed into life, the present cannot become the past, nothing can ever change.

There is a purpose to sunlight in everything it touches.

Father Sabino's eyes reflected the sunlight as he took his first steps through Mãe Luíza.

He looked closely at the open ditches, filled with scraps of food and feces. The scent of urine was everywhere, as were the malnourished children, some with bruises and sores on their bodies, playing near the garbage. He saw the old people, unassisted, dying faster and more sadly in untended gardens, forgotten in the alleyways. The children pretended not to see him, or, if they did, acted as if he had lived there for a long time.

He saw public school students talking on street corners, street-sellers loudly advertising their products for the poor, people sitting in the sun as they convalesced from numerous illnesses. This was a Mãe Luíza with no designs for a better future, a slum like any other in Brazil. Except that almost all of its population, having escaped the droughts, was now submerged in the rotten life offered by the Brazilian state.

Sabino entered a corner shop that sold alcohol, sweets and other cheap products. It was the regular meeting point for a group of heavy drinkers. Some talked about football, others were lying on the floor, completely inebriated. After a hearty "hello" he asked for a beer. The men replied almost in unison, automatically, without looking him in the eyes. People came and went at that shop, so the men greeted anyone who arrived, not noticing that this man was different from everyone else.

Sabino turned towards the corner shop entrance. As he observed the comings and goings, he noticed men in suits and ties preaching the Gospel from door to door, alongside people walking around with not much to do. He knew about Father João Perestrello and Father Costa. He asked a passerby where their community center was. She offered him an assured and detailed explanation of how to get there. She added that her eldest son had studied there. She would have wanted her youngest to do the same, but the place had been shut down for some time.

Sabino paid for his beer and followed the woman's directions. He inspected the place discreetly, because a family was now living in what was once the community center. It was a small room considering the number of children playing in the yard. He tried to imagine what could have gone so wrong that the priests felt they had to abandon their community work.

He had first come across children from Mãe Luíza as they sold their sweets outside the Salesian school. It was from them that he first learned about the frightful state of the place. He knew then that he would have to buy a big house to be able to do some good in that neighborhood. He had in his heart a huge desire to be helpful. He did not know how he was going to act on it, but he was certain that if he did not take a first step, he would not be able to move forward, towards the future that the sun has in store for all our lives.

He continued walking around the neighborhood until he came across a large house that he liked. It was strategically located, and he wondered whether the owners might sell it. He clapped hands in front of the gate and some children came out to greet him. They said their parents were at work and would only come back at night.

Sabino sat on a bench in a small square, looking around like someone simply watching time go by. It was late 1979. He could picture the pain that had inhabited those alleys, those poorly built houses, those paths down which so many helpless and abandoned children ran, playing, unaware that they were unhappy.

He took all of it in, but in reality he was imagining what he might be able to do by working with the community. Helping everything and everyone is what makes life flourish.

Sabino was like that, one of those people who live astride poetry, philosophy and action. His heart rose above everything, even above the many gods from the various religions of mankind. Sabino, a Christian, was sensitive to people and to their multiple views of God. He respected and truly loved human's differing perceptions of the sacred. For him, that was more meaningful than religions themselves. He became an authority among Catholics and non-Catholics on matters of theology, and he saw his pastoral work as applying to all. In his view of Christianity, the church should be concerned with all people.

He felt hungry around two in the afternoon. He went back to the corner shop, asked for a mortadella sandwich. He felt like having another beer.

He had found the house he wanted, right in the middle of the neighborhood. If he were able to buy it, that is where he would build his church. He had asked to step down as head of the Salesian school, in Natal. When children from Mãe Luíza told him about the sad state of the neighborhood, he decided he was going to live there to help change that reality, whatever it took. To remain at the Salesian school, engaging with only a few individuals, would not help much. He had to go to where the people were, be part of their daily lives.

The owner of the house arrived with her husband, carrying bags filled with their shopping. He decided not to talk to them then. He would wait for the man to clean up and head for the corner shop to drink a cachaça and work up an appetite, as most of the working people in the place did. But nobody came out, so Sabino decided to leave.

He returned to Mãe Luíza over the next few days, not revealing he was a priest, and his visits became a habit. He befriended some of those who frequented the local bars, who loitered on street corners, or outside schools. People only found out he was a priest because of the children he had spoken to outside the Salesian school.

Sabino gave up on his plans to buy the house he had liked when he realized that the family was well established there, and that the owner had plans to expand and build two more rooms.

He found out that another priest owned a house in Mãe Luíza but kept it shut. Sabino tracked him down to a church in a nearby neighborhood, where he was being looked after by other priests. That other priest had wanted to build a church in Mãe Luíza, but he was afflicted by a serious disease and was unable to carry out his project. The father wanted to donate the property to Sabino, who insisted on paying, because that way he might help the priest in his illness. Sabino fixed up the little house and made it his home.

From that day on, he prayed with people on street corners wearing his priest's cassock, he went to schools, lectured, visited the sick, took them to the doctor, gave food to the needy, processed through Ribeira on holy days, spoke to Zé Pelintra, Dona Maria Padilha and Seu Tranca-Rua in the *umbanda* grounds. On Friday nights he went to Seu Mané's *forrós*, and he danced with all the unaccompanied women. He also went to the police station to help release people who had been arrested for not carrying identification. Sabino helped people fight for their rights.

Over time he got to know the women's prayer group, the managers of the homeless shelters, and the missionaries. He lit big bonfires for the feasts of St. Peter and St. John. He organized community walks on the days of the Fraternity Campaign, which always had a social-political theme. The prostitutes at the Ribeira brothel gravitated towards Sabino's activities – many even left their trade. His intention was not only to practice charity, but to fight for a better life for everyone.

Sabino had a sense of humor. He watched the *telenovelas* on Globo TV to better understand and communicate with people. He was Italian, but could easily pass for Brazilian because he did not have a foreign accent, he was always playful, and loved making a joke of everything. He made every person feel like the most important human being on the planet. He always had time for everyone, and rebuked no one.

He also came to an arrangement with the drug dealers. He asked them to lower the volume on their sound systems when they had a party, and not to set off fireworks in front of his house to announce the arrival of a drug shipment. He gained their respect, and even asked them to help return items stolen from within their community. Whenever there was a robbery, the gang members helped restore stolen items to their rightful owners.

When Italian or German visitors came to see him, he took them along to witness the *umbanda* rituals and, if they felt like it, to take part. He was fascinated by the sacred in all religions.

He became well known to the local authorities, including magistrates and judges. Working with someone from the local university, together with residents and architectural experts, he helped draft a law that would protect Mãe Luíza by including it in Natal's urban planning strategy. Also with the residents he organized the groups that would transform the rickety wooden shacks in the Sopapo neighborhood into brick and breeze-block houses.

Both within Brazil and abroad, Sabino had the support of many people who contributed financially to his work, but still the Catholic church and the government refused to help him.

Later, with the help of Seu Cabral, a fervent Catholic, he bought another house, which he turned into a chapel. Seu Cabral, who helped the priest in his community work, was hoping to buy the adjoining properties to increase the size of the church and build a community center, but even before that happened, there were services taking place daily in the small chapel. The place had an altar with a cross and images of saints. It also had wooden benches for the older people to sit on. The services reflected on life in the community, on its moments of happiness and sadness, on its injustices and hopes. Sabino passed his theological knowledge on to young and old, who took it all in quietly, and felt driven to fight for a better life in an unfair society. Yes, Christ was there in the form of political conscience.

One day, however, Seu Cabral became an Evangelical Christian. Other Evangelicals came by the chapel every day, when Sabino was not around, to try to influence him and offer him benefits if the place were to become an Evangelical church instead.

Seu Cabral resisted for some time, until the day he took the cross and the images of saints and threw them all out, saying they were the devil's work. Sabino went to deliver his service as usual. He was startled to see the cross and the images of saints lying on the ground.

The faithful who had gone to attend Sabino's mass were horrified by the crowd of men in suits and the women in long dresses arriving at the chapel. Sabino entered the temple, and his followers came in behind him. Inside, a pastor was preaching against Catholicism. According to Christ, he was saying, it is a sin to adore images, so in the name of the Lord the chapel had now become an Evangelical church. Calmly, Father Sabino asked for permission to speak and rallied the faithful:

"Whoever wants to remain a Catholic can follow me."

Many people followed the priest, who then delivered his mass on the street, as if nothing had happened, and without once mentioning the name of the man who had become an Evangelical pastor overnight. After a week, Seu Cabral went to Sabino's house to pay back the money the priest had invested in the purchase of the land and in building the chapel.

After a lot of coaxing and cajoling, the mayor's office agreed to give Sabino a large plot of land, located strategically near the center of the neighborhood.

Sabino had friends who were architects and engineers, and they agreed to oversee the building of the new church. A battalion of volunteers made itself available for the building work. Men, women and children, the old and the young, people of all sorts helped build the church while in parallel they attempted to build a world of social justice – two things that Sabino considered inseparable. Meanwhile, Sabino continued his social work and established a community center he called the Centro Sócio-Pastoral Nossa Senhora da Conceição.

Sabino's family, alongside his German, Italian, Swiss and Brazilian friends, helped him financially in this first phase, and the building work proceeded at full speed. Sometimes work was paused due to delays with the funding, but nothing interrupted it for too long.

While the work was ongoing, Seu Cabral and Marco Nanuki – another Catholic turned Evangelical – approached the priest with a check for 20,000 cruzeiros. Sabino was delivering his mass on the building site. Seu Oscar, a friend of Sabino, ripped up the check and handed the scraps of paper back to the two men.

The main building work was finished a few months later. The church was called the chapel of Nossa Senhora da Conceição de Mãe Luíza. The day the roof was put into place, there was a party in Mãe Luíza the likes of which had never been seen. People brought whatever food or drink they could in a celebration that lasted through the night. Sabino was one of the few people to remain sober: he could hold his drink, like many Italians, and it was as if he had not even had a sip of alcohol. People asked if a priest was allowed to drink, to which he replied, with a twinkle in his eye: "Of course!"

The final stages of the building work were fast and enjoyable. The community center, attached to the church, now included a nursery and a school for adult learners, as requested by the community. The place was now filled with people. The teachers were local residents, often studying themselves, who, without any formal training or qualifications, had offered to teach others out of love and solidarity.

Sister Anatólia was from the city of Santa Cruz, in the state's interior. The daughter of a Catholic family – one of seven sisters – she had decided very early in life that she would dedicate herself to a life of religion. She was ordained in 1964. When Father Sabino decided to go to Mãe Luíza, he stopped by the College of Maria

Auxiliadora, near the neighborhood, to ask the sisters for their help in the task of setting up a Catholic church. The sisters bought a small house near the chapel of Nossa Senhora da Conceição, which was being built, and stayed there for two years. After that period, they returned to the College, but Sister Anatólia stayed behind in Mãe Luíza and became Father Sabino's right-hand person in anything to do with the church.

Sister Anatólia earned the entire community's affection. It was she who advised the old and the young about the many challenges they faced.

A youth group was formed at the Centro Sócio-Pastoral. Its members were keen to participate, and often argued noisily about who might coordinate their activities. Vitória was one of the people drawn to the group, but she did not like the constant arguing. She was a young woman, and did not want to be stuck with those loud and lively teenage boys who laughed about the silliest things, so she did not return until the school opened. Only then, with the coordinators formally appointed, did Vitória and Inês start attending classes.

Vitória did not miss a single lesson, but what she liked most was learning about politics. She was delighted when the Pastoral Operária, or Workers Pastoral, was founded. When Father Sabino organized a worker's demonstration on May 1, demanding higher pay and better working conditions in local factories, she pledged never to abandon the fight for social justice.

Vitória and Inês approached Sabino at the Pastoral Operária. Vitória was already part of the teachers' union. She was not a practicing Catholic, but she preferred the verb "to be" to the verb "to have." This distinction was at the heart of her outlook and her political engagement. She was upset by the long queues of people waiting to register their children for school at the Centro Sócio-Pastoral. She was appalled to see mothers standing in line for two days to get their children a place in the local public school – to no avail.

So, together with colleagues from the Pastoral, she helped found the Workers' Party in Natal. To raise funds, she sold beer at parties. At one of those parties, after the bar had closed, she ended up drinking with Sabino. She realized she had found her place. She would become the head educator at the Centro Sócio-Pastoral's preschool called Espaço Livre, or Free Space.

Inês was enthusiastic and smart, and she decided to join the Pastoral Operária founded by Father Sabino and Vitória. She had studied history, had gained teaching qualifications and taught at a local public school. At the Centro Sócio-Pastoral she would be in charge of Casa Crescer – A House for Growth – the school that would support children who were struggling with their regular education.

Largely thanks to her efforts, and to what she had learned working in Mãe Luíza, the municipal school at which Inês worked was widely considered one of the city's best public schools. Always discreet, Inês was a key person at the Centro.

One of the biggest problems at Mãe Luíza was infant mortality. When he met Gabriela, Sabino asked for her help. She was the cousin of a friend, she worked as a family health worker in her country, and was spending a sabbatical year in Brazil.

Gabriela went into Mãe Luíza one morning, saw the pain in the eyes of its people, and understood why Sabino has asked for her help. The word of Christ, to those who believe in it, must be put into practice, and she admired what Sabino was doing. Soon after, accompanied by people in the community, Gabriela was visiting pregnant women and families with babies. Gabriela threw herself into her work while the priest bought supplies for the families in need, hoping to diminish child mortality. On her days off, she sold crafts to contribute to the church's expenses.

Bentinho had studied medicine. His days of student politics were now behind him, and he was longing for new causes to embrace. He was walking across Praça Padre João Maria when he saw Gabriela trying to speak Portuguese to potential buyers, in an effort to sell the educational toys and crafts made in Mãe Luíza. Love can strike at any time and in any place. When she saw him, she was left speechless. The world stood still for them both. After the initial jolt, he said hello in French, and she responded with the smile of a woman struck by love at first sight. He stuck around, helping her communicate with her customers.

Bentinho was a Marxist. He had inherited his ideas about social equality from his father, a union organizer who had been fired from Petrobras when the dictatorship took over the country. Bentinho was a young idealist. He wanted all human beings to feel socially included. Gabriela became the woman of his life: they agreed on everything, and felt in sync with each other like they had never felt before. They knew that one only loves once in this life. Despite her being religious and him being a non-believer, they found they shared the same purpose in life.

Soon after, Bentinho started offering pediatric consultations in a place near the church. He suggested to Father Sabino that they organize a community meeting about children's health. That way, they might be able to talk to residents about the difficult issue of infant mortality. Many good ideas sprang from that event. One of them was the suggestion that regular health visits to pregnant women and mothers with newborn babies might be carried out in collaboration with mothers from the neighborhood. The initiative was called Projeto Amigos da Comunidade, or Friends of the Community Project. For Bentinho, the work in Mãe Luíza was a continuation of the work he had done as a student leader.

Bentinho, Gabriela and Sabino, each with his or her own expertise, trained visiting health workers who administered vaccines, managed respiratory diseases, and advised mothers on breastfeeding, weaning and infant nutrition. There were twelve visits per year for every family, one a month, and Vitória asked to join in that work too.

Úrsula met Father Sabino in June of 1980. She was in a hospital bed, depressed and stricken with pneumonia. A ward sister, who knew of Sabino's spiritual influence, called him in to speak to Úrsula, who promptly recovered and went on to finish her odontology course. Later, at a Mothers' Day mass in Mãe Luíza, Sabino asked her to help clean and bandage the wounds of a local woman who was suffering from breast cancer.

Úrsula grew very close to Sabino, who shared with her his personal worries as well as his concerns about the progress of his community work.

After another community meeting, which they called Mãe Luíza Looks After Its Aged, focusing on the issues of the elderly, the group came up with another project – Espaço Solidário, or A Space for Solidarity. Its purpose was to offer support to old people who were in need, hungry, abandoned by their families, alcohol abusers, homeless, sick.

There were many elderly people begging on the streets, left to their own misfortune. For instance, nobody in her family wanted Lucinda at home. She was an alcoholic. So, she was thrown out to live on the streets and rummage through the garbage for food. Even after she was welcomed in the Espaço Solidário, it took more than a year for her to understand that she now had a new home. She still believed that she was meant to be on the streets, so the volunteers from the Espaço had to go and find her when she left, and bring her back to the shelter. Years later, Lucinda's family life had been revived, with her relatives visiting her at the Espaço Solidário.

Gabriela oversaw social care visits. She worked closely with the families to ensure that old people's circumstances were better.

Many residents arrived at the Espaço Solidário to speak out against the atrocious conditions in which some elderly people lived – some were even tied to chairs. There were horrifying cases. Sometimes it became necessary to involve the Public Prosecutor's office. But such abuse stopped happening as a new culture of care for the elderly developed, thanks to conversations between the Centro Sócio-Pastoral and the community. Inspired by Sabino's ideas, the Espaço Solidário's architectural design made it a house open to all.

When the Amigos da Comunidade project came to an end, Sabino hired all the health workers who used to visit expectant and new mothers to work at the Espaço Solidário. Infant mortality was a thing of the past. The biggest worry now was the elderly. Sabino did everything he could to keep the initiative going. At the Espaço, old people had access to food, recreation and socialization, as well as medical and psychological support. They also received the warmth, affection and peace so lovingly offered by that group of people, hailing from such different places, backgrounds and cultures. Even Bentinho, a non-believer, had started wondering whether it might have been God who brought those people together. He was beginning to show signs of faith because there were things that science could not explain.

The only time Father Sabino asked to spend a day and a night on his own was when his father died, back in Italy. He knew that his father had died a happy man because he had a son like him, but he would have wanted to hold his father in his final hours. Since he arrived at Mãe Luíza, Sabino had visited his father a few times. They had laughed and joked, and Sabino had told his father about his work in Brazil. His father looked well, and was seemingly in good health, but he died suddenly. Sabino was alone in his house when he heard the news. He prayed to God that, if he really existed, he might welcome his own father into heaven. The following day he said a mass for his father, and then immediately flew off to be with his family.

There was a party for him upon his return: it was 13 July, his birthday. But it was he who came bearing gifts for the residents of Mãe Luíza.

Ana, her father and her brother believed that – given the high living standards in Switzerland – they ought to give something back to society, particularly to those who had the least. They created the APOREMA Foundation, which focused on humanitarian help.

In the late eighties, Ana and her brother met a European couple who was travelling to Brazil to do humanitarian work in Rio Grande do Norte. The Foundation supported the couple's project, which was dedicated to the production of cashew nuts.

The couple knew Sabino, and helped him with some of his projects in Mãe Luíza. They had plans to work together on improving people's nutrition and health, and to help children with Down's Syndrome improve their achievement in school. They set up a small workshop for the production of hand-crafted toys, the sale of which would provide the makers a small income.

In the early nineties, APOREMA started supporting the couple's work in Mãe Luíza. This led to the creation of Casa Crescer in 1993. The name was chosen by Sabino. Over time, APOREMA's support extended to all of the Centro Sócio-Pastoral's work.

During that time, Sabino and Ana become closer. They understood each other profoundly, and fully accepted one another as they were. A great trust grew between them, which led to a truly unique friendship. Today, Ana still remembers the many moments spent with Sabino, as he shared his countless ideas, visions, doubts and worries.

When she first met Sabino's work team, Ana had the feeling that she had known them for years. They were in sync, they shared the same happiness and the same truth: they were all people of goodwill and big dreams, who wanted for every human being the things that were essential to human dignity – things that the powers that be, on the right of the political spectrum, had refused to offer for as long as Brazil had been Brazil.

Coming from abroad, Ana brought different perspectives that led to innumerable discussions which, in the end, were always constructive and fruitful.

She did not lose heart when her camera and her handbag with all its contents were stolen during a robber in Mãe Luíza. As he knew all the criminals in the neighborhood, Father Sabino had some idea of who might have done it. He knocked on the thief's door and made him retrieve the camera, which he had already sold, and returned it to Ana. That was the spirit of the place.

By then, Sabino Gentili already knew that his fight would continue even after he was no longer there himself. He felt that the people he had gathered around him would not abandon the project they had developed together. He saw many of the children who had come to his school when he first opened it, early on in his journey, now grown up and working in other community projects, going to university, some already graduated, others already employed, living with a dignity they may never have achieved otherwise.

Sabino saw the sacred in people's lives and suffered alongside those people steeped in poverty, but he was, nevertheless, a happy and confident man, a rock strengthened by his pain and his perplexed faith. He was determined to spread the word of Christ because he wanted to share, as Christ had done. Sharing, for Sabino, meant offering everyone equal parts. Not charity, which means giving away a little part of what we have, not helping out for only a moment, but a true division of material goods, of spiritual goods, of knowledge, a division that is just and enduring. Sharing is a form of communion, allowing us all to be the same, whether we are illuminated by the sun or not.

Father Sabino died on July 8, 2006 as a result of heart problems. He was in the town of his birth, in Italy. He knew his heart was too big and that there was no cure for the problem. It was a heart larger than the world. It harbored more love than anyone else's, more fraternity, more certainty of better times ahead for all, no matter what race, ethnicity or skin color.

He saw people fighting to keep alive the projects he had created, so he did not mind dying. There were so many more people doing good work with a new awareness of class, with knowledge of history, with the drive to ensure the community's well-being.

Anticipating his death, he said his farewells happily. He wanted to see his relatives again, to walk once more over the ground of his childhood, go back to where it all began.

Sabino died on the day of the procession for Sant'Anatolia, patron saint of the town of Castel di Tora. That same morning, he had followed the procession himself, only to die a few hours later. Friends came from far away to bid a fond farewell to the old fighter who had left the world in the town where he had first entered it. That was the moment when Bentinho, Vitória, Úrsula and Gabriela first met and befriended Ana. Also present at that momentous event were Sabino's German and Swiss friends. That was the origin of an unshakeable international partnership.

Sabino was gone, but his working methods had taken root. It was the community that suggested what needed to be done. Now that many of the vital needs of Mãe Luíza's residents had been met, the work had to continue: it was necessary to continue listening to the community and working to meet the challenges it saw. The team never doubted that they had to carry on, they never considered stopping. Keeping up the work came naturally.

So, it went on, and the people realized they needed spaces that were appropriate for life, for sport, for leisure, for culture and for art.

The team threw itself into the renewed efforts, adding new pieces to the jigsaw in a struggle that will continue until Brazil is governed by people who genuinely listen to its population and make the country a just and egalitarian nation.

There is hope that the sun will shine once again, in a future filled with promise for all, in Brazil and across the rest of the world. One day we will all be happy, forever showered by the grace of every ray of light from the sun, the moon and the stars.

Preta - Trampolim
Jaci-Nyar

Mãe Luíza
Building Optimism

Foreword

It goes without saying that whenever we encounter wrongs and inequities we should try to remedy the situation. This is especially the case when the standard of living is in glaring contrast to our own personal values and notions of human dignity. Regardless of the causation involved, the will to help others is innately human. And beyond merely providing emergency aid, we often aspire to bring about lasting change as well.

This publication presents detailed documentation of a project that has its origins in our own ethical and moral convictions. Our endeavor inevitably started out with an analysis and critique of the causes of the grievances in question. A weak state, failed policies, a history of discrimination, and the marginalization of entire ethnic groups have resulted in many people being forced to expend all their energy on mere survival—by pursuing activities remote from their actual talents and resources, let alone their true desires. This is an intolerable state of affairs that can be encountered in many parts of the world where the fight against poverty and its effects is not making much progress.

The fact that the district of Mãe Luíza in the Brazilian state of Rio Grande do Norte has managed to bring about a modicum of normality to replace the once miserable conditions can be attributed to the fact that those involved were in agreement from the start that the primary, albeit distant, goal to be pursued was community building and fostering civic spirit, and that this would be a gradual development over several generations.

At the beginning of a process that lasted 30 years, all efforts were geared toward the struggle for survival, to ensure the safety, health, and sustenance of the people affected. Once these basic requirements had been met, attention shifted to broader needs: for community, education, culture, self-fulfillment, and integration for as many inhabitants of Mãe Luíza as possible.

This success story is the result of a coincidental meeting of personalities with similar attitudes and ideas. Father Sabino, an Italian priest known by his faithful as Padre Sabino, was perhaps moved to choose this setting for his work in 1979 due to the glaring accumulation of abuses he found there. His charisma and initiatives attracted like-minded individuals, who contributed their expertise and financial support to the undertaking.

Measures were introduced to curb the high child mortality and ensure adequate healthcare and water supply. This was followed by interventions in the educational system and the provision of space and staff for schools for both children and adults, along with care for the elderly. The process crept forward over the years in small but steady steps and, even after Padre Sabino's death in 2006, was able to rely on the structures he had put in place. The inhabitants of Mãe Luíza had developed a sense of belonging. Under these premises, it was possible to address the question of how the sprawling suburban structure of the district could be consolidated by establishing features that would help to create a visible identity for it. Interventions were made in public space and traffic management, and access to the sea was ensured; a "green street" was established, an arena was built, and a music school was founded.

This book documents the measures that turned a slum district into a lively community. Paulo Lins sets the tone with his moving narrative. Mô Bleeker provides the socio-political background, proposing the figure of the spiral as symbol for the future and for the optimism that has allowed Mãe Luíza to become what it is today – an example for others to follow.

We dedicate this book to the many people who through their perseverance and confidence have helped build this spiral, and to the citizens of Mãe Luíza who keep it constantly in motion.

The Editors

Atlantic Ocean

0°

23° S

0   250   500   1000 km

State of Rio Grande do Norte in Brazil

35

Atlantic Ocean

0   25   50   100 km

Natal and its Metropolitan Area in the state of Rio Grande do Norte

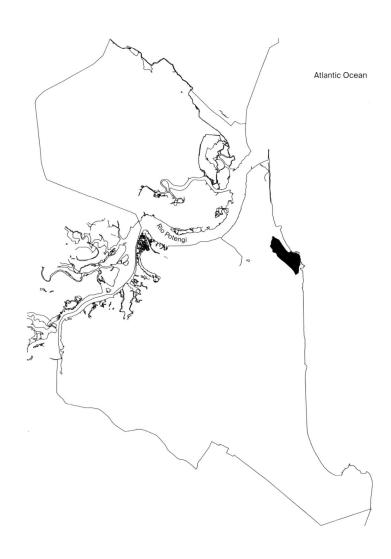

Atlantic Ocean

Rio Potengi

0   1   2.5   5 km

Mãe Luíza in Natal

Atlantic Ocean

50 100 250 m

Mãe Luíza

Ion de Andrade

Origin of the Settlement

Social exclusion, climate factors, and the growth of the construction industry shaped the development of the Mãe Luíza neighborhood during Brazil's period of rural exodus. Settlement was arduous, with no support from public authorities, in an area that was difficult to get to and which lacked even basic sanitation.

The urbanization process in Brazil began in the late 1940s and early 1950s as a result of the increased rate of industrialization throughout the country. According to the Brazilian Institute of Geography and Statistics (IBGE), Brazil's urban population made up 36.5% of the country's total population in 1950 and exceeded 70% by the 1980s. Two industries led the push towards urbanization: the automotive industry, which attracted Brazilians of all origins to the Rio–São Paulo axis, and the civil construction industry, which produced, above all, a migration from Brazil's rural interior to its capital cities.

Another factor played an important role in the emigration of Northeastern farmers, and it was typically Northeastern, although cyclical in nature: the droughts. It is possible that none of the displacement would have occurred were it not for the poverty and social exclusion experienced at that time in Brazil's rural areas.

Mãe Luíza was settled during the period known as the "rural exodus." The neighborhood was officially registered January 23, 1958, in accordance with Law 794.

Settlement of this rural population into the urban environments took place in the absence of government support. Like in so many other Brazilian cities, Mãe Luíza was selected because it was in a hard-to-reach area, where unpopulated hills were covered with dense vegetation. The earliest residents and their families had to use machetes to clear their way through the trees.

On top of those hills they built their earthen floor houses using wattle and daub, and straw. Most had no bathrooms and water was only available in some parts of the neighborhood or when donated by people from the neighboring Petrópolis. Women and children would use 10-liter cans to carry water home on top of their heads. Only in 1971 was Mãe Luíza's first water reservoir installed.

No one can deny how much this settlement suffered, especially over the loss of its elderly and infants, who endured starvation, thirst, and disease for many years.

Today's Green Street, ca. 1960

Rua João XXIII, ca. 1960

Areia Preta Beach, ca. 1950

Areia Preta Beach with the Mãe Luíza Lighthouse, in the 1950s

Areia Preta Beach, ca. 1950

Mãe Luíza viewed from the Lighthouse, ca. 1960 › Rua Aluízio Alvez, 1997

Tomislav Dushanov

Arriving in Mãe Luíza

The region's distinctive landscapes accompany visitors to Mãe Luíza. Dunes, thorny bushes, dense trees, and the constant ocean breeze lead to this neighborhood, known for its friendly residents, despite chronic poverty and adversity common to poorer housing areas.

94

One can arrive in Mãe Luíza from either downtown Natal or the ocean side. The latter approach, along the Via Costeira, offers a more beautiful ride between the ocean and the dunes, presenting an uninterrupted panoramic view of the area's main natural features.

There are no islands off Natal and usually no ships in sight, thus allowing a distant view of the horizon. Because it is Brazil's closest point to Europe, the site was one of the early and central arrival points for Europeans traveling to Brazil and other parts of South America. The beach at Mãe Luíza feels like deserted urban coastline compared to popular nearby resorts and remains the closest and most readily available recreational area for the neighborhood.

The dunes along the highway are naturally protected zones of vast sand hills, covered with thorny bushes and dense trees. The unusual combination of sand and vegetation reflects the unique character of this part of the country, where semi-arid and tropical landscapes meet.

From the vastness along the Via Costeira, the road turns sharply up into the dunes, away from the ocean, and enters the narrow streets and vibrant crowds of Mãe Luíza. The neighborhood, a dense settlement in a spectacular natural setting, has remained compact and preserved its natural surroundings, with lush green as its constant backdrop and sand as its fragile floor. The densely packed small houses with miniature windows and colorful walls are protected from the equatorial sun by a cover of ubiquitous red tiled roofs.

The resulting homogeneous urban tissue is cut in two by the main street, Rua João XXIII. Here the church, the Centro Sócio, small shops, bakeries, grocery stores, DVD rentals, cafes, repair shops, and bus stops form a natural gathering place for the community. The street has been undergoing an urban facelift, evident in refurbished sidewalks, a small marketplace, and a lot of new landscaping, compliments of the municipality and locals. But unfinished street lighting serves as longstanding witness to how difficult and slowly improvements arrive to such underprivileged areas.

From the main road stem myriad short side streets, which offer a very different and quieter sense of proximity, homogeneity and privacy. In these narrow alleys reigns the somewhat disquiet feeling of isolated outdoor spaces claimed by the residents, who open their living rooms toward the sidewalk to add space, daylight and a bit of fresh air. The side streets end directly at the dunes, where one can climb the sandy forest floor to get an unobstructed view of Mãe Luíza and beyond to downtown Natal with its low-rise houses, sporadic towers and giant white bridge over the Potengi River.

Among the clustered ordinary buildings, one encounters a few out-standing structures, which create centers of activity and prominence in the neighborhood. Most visible is the old Lighthouse, the Farol, which uses the high dunes to raise itself above all of Natal, offering a sweeping view of the city and the ocean.

Across the street from the Farol is the Arena do Morro gymnasium. Its large white roof over the school playground, lit like a lantern at night, is hard to miss. In the seven years since it opened, the building has become much more than an athletic field, accommodating educational, sports, cultural and community activities from early morning to late evening, and it is where public appeal, sheer size and the constant breeze of cool fresh air converge to bring something of the ocean grandness to the small scale of the neighborhood.

Between the two flows of the principal street lies the main square, where one can find the church and Centro Sócio buildings that have grown together. The local market, outdoor exercise space, expansive natural greenery along the street, as well as the oft-heard melodies from the nearby Music School complete the feeling of neighborhood center.

From here one can reach the beach by way of the Grand Stairs, a monumental structure of interwoven steps and ramps built on the site of the massive 2014 landslide that pushed many houses into the ocean. That unfortunate natural disaster was able to penetrate the wall of high-end residential towers along the beach and directly connect the heart of Mãe Luíza to the ocean.

One does well to remember that this neighborhood experience is different from other similar areas. Remarkably, the people of Mãe Luíza have built an atmosphere of openness and warmth, despite chronic poverty, and regardless of the adversity of the place, they have learned to respond with distinct friendliness, hospitality and care.

Historical Milestones

Since the early 1980s, the Centro Sócio has been contributing in the areas of education, health, citizenship, urbanization, sports, and culture through partnerships with public and private entities and with community participation in the projects aimed at development and social inclusion.

Projects initiated by the Centro Sócio

	Projects	Additional Information	Discontinued / Reason / Date
1981	Construction of the church	Rua João XXIII Initiated by Padre Sabino Gentili	
12/8/1983	Legal foundation of the Centro Sócio	Located in the church's annex	
5/31/1986	Opening of the Espaço Livre preschool	4ª Trav. João XXIII, 89 Preschool for childhood literacy that serves up to 190 students aged 3–5. From 1986–1990, the building also served as a school for adult literacy that could hold 50.	
1990	Casa da Criança daycare center	Rua João XXIII (across from the Catholic church). It served children with malnutrition (feeding them once a day) and also offered daily pediatric consultations and monthly meetings with the mothers. The Friends of the Community project was launched after the neighborhood's high infant mortality rate was observed.	Discontinued in 2001 when the Friends of the Community project ended. Pediatric visits continue to take place in an office at the Espaço Solidário eldercare center.
1991	Friends of the Community project	Project involving 10 neighborhood health visitors. They visited pregnant women and followed the mothers through their child's first birthday. Objective: Limit infant mortality by encouraging breastfeeding and provide guidance on prevention and care in case of dehydration, malnutrition, diarrhea, pneumonia, and other issues.	Discontinued in 2001 after the municipal Community Health Agents Program was implemented linked to neighborhood health centers.
1991	Escola Novo Lar literacy center	Adult literacy course at the Centro Sócio (two sections of 30 students).	Discontinued in 2004 when the public school began to offer classes to young people and adults.
5/17/1993	Casa Crescer educational center	10ª Trav. João XXIII, N° 10 Serves up to 190 children aged 7–15 in the after-school program designed for children with learning disabilities. It is also a place for continuing education for the children of working mothers. Casa Crescer actively searches for children and young people who drop out of school. It conducts music, sports, and digital inclusion activities. Objective: reinforce and contribute to improved reading and writing.	

1993	Educational space for children with special needs	It was opened at the Casa Crescer by Mrs. Elisabeth Raboud and then continued in a classroom at the Espaço Livre preschool. It served children aged 6–15.	Discontinued in 2012. The children were mainstreamed into public schools and received comprehensive care at the CRI (Child Rehabilitation Center).
1995	Urban land dispute	With Prof. Dulce Bentes from the Department of Architecture at the Federal University of Rio Grande do Norte (UFRN), first neighborhood to be recognized as a Special Area of Social Interest within the Natal Master Plan, through passage of Law 4.663.	An ongoing struggle since the Master Plan is revised every 10 years.
1996	Urbanization of the Favela do Sopapo (Brisa do Mar Housing Project)	Rua Camaragibe Project borne out of the 1993 Fraternity Campaign on the topic "Fraternity and Housing," whose motto was: "Where do you live?" The project lasted five years with weekly meetings and resulted in the group effort to construct 60 houses. Objective: building harmony, fulfilling dreams, and affirming dignity.	1999–2000 Completion of construction and occupation of houses.
08/2001	Espaço Solidário eldercare center	Rua Largo do Farol, N° 36 Long-term Residential Institution for the Elderly (ILPI), eldercare and social center. Developed after the Friends of the Community project ended. Its former visitors were hired as caregivers to those identified as at-risk elderly with no alternative shelters. Today it serves 23 residents of both sexes and 37 daycare participants (2019).	
2004	Computer Technology School	A Centro Sócio initiative put in place after discontinuation of the Escola Novo Lar literacy center. Objective: Prepare young people in Mãe Luíza for the job market.	
4/9/2014	Arena do Morro gymnasium	Rua Camaragibe Each week, it serves an average of 1,200 youth and adults (including students who attend the State Public School Senador Dinarte Mariz) for activities like soccer, basketball, rhythmic gymnastics, handball, badminton, karate, taekwondo, or nighttime pickup soccer. Besides these regular activities, the gymnasium is a venue for occasional cultural and other events.	Construction: 2012–2014 Opened in 2014.
2016	Brass Band	Composed of 35 members on average	
4/28/2018	Espaço Livre Music School	4ª Trav. João XXIII, 89 Serves 75 students	Construction: 2016–2018 Opened in 2018.
2021	Publication of the book *Mãe Luíza – Building Optimism* with the story "Creating a New Sun" by Paulo Lins		Begun in 2018 About the development of Mãe Luíza

108 **Projects initiated by the government and other entities**

	Project	Additional Information	Observations
1940s	Settlement (birth of the neighborhood)		
1950s	Cacimba do Pinto / Areia Preta	First water supply point for residents of the Mãe Luíza neighborhood and community laundry site used by the neighborhood's women.	Implemented by the Natal City Government
1951	Lighthouse		Built by the Navy
1/23/1958	Official foundation of the neighborhood of Mãe Luíza	Municipal Law 794/1958	Implemented by the Natal City Government
1960–1970	Electricity	1960s: street lighting 1970s: electricity reaches houses of residents of the neighborhood	Implemented by the Natal City Government
1964	State Public School Monsenhor Alfredo Pegado	Rua João XXIII, 603	Implemented by the State Government.
1965	Padre Perestrello Social Center	Rua João XXIII Develops leisure activities for the community. Venue for meetings for the elderly and games. Organizes events and assistance for people experiencing difficulties. Provides space for the community to mourn its dead.	Community Association
1967	Fountain	Located on the site currently occupied by the Catholic church. Serves as water supply to neighborhood residents. Water paid by the gallon, barrel, or load (cart with several barrels).	Implemented by the Natal City Government
9/6/1968	State Public School Selva Capistrano Lopes da Silva	Rua Guanabara, 147	Implemented by the State Government
1971	Water reservoir	Rua São Pedro	Implemented by the Natal City Government
5/2/1974	Soccer field / Mãe Luíza and Aparecida Sports Center	Rua João XXIII, 1278 Soccer training with tournaments between organized teams in the neighborhood. Space provided for development of the "Beacons of the Future" project for the community's children.	Community Association

Date	Project	Location	Implementation
3/15/1976	Rua João XXIII Healthcare Post	Rua João XXIII	Implemented by the Natal City Government
5/3/1976	Establishment of the Community Council	Rua João XXIII	Community Association
1977	State Public School Prof. Severino Bezerra de Melo	Rua João XXIII	Implemented by the State Government. Remodeled in 2020.
1978–1979	Arrival of the bus line	Line 40	Implemented by the Natal City Government
1/12/1982	Padre João Perestrello Day Care Center	Rua João XXIII, 729	Implemented by the Natal City Government
1983	Police Station	Rua João XXIII	Implemented by the State Government
1985	Construction of the Pro-morar Housing Project	Rua São Francisco and Rua Bartolomeu Ferraz Objective: Relocate people living in high-risk areas on the slopes of the neighborhood.	Project of the National Council for Urban Development, funded by the National Housing Bank. Completed.
1986	State Public School Senador Dinarte Mariz	Rua Camaragibe	Implemented by the State Government. Remodeled in 2020.
1988	Guanabara Healthcare Post	Basic Health Unit Rua Guanabara	Implemented by the Natal City Government
The 1990s	Police Station, 4th Precinct	Rua João XXIII	Implemented by the State Government
06/1992	Municipal Public School Prof. Antônio Campos e Silva	Rua João XXIII, 1821	Implemented by the Natal City Government
8/16/1996	Municipal Daycare Center Galdina Barbosa Silveira Guimarães (CMEI)	Rua João XXIII, 1719	Implemented by the Natal City Government
2010	Basic sanitation / sewage system		Implemented by the Natal City Government with federal funds
2013	Green Street	Alameda Padre Sabino Gentili Part of the "A Vision for Mãe Luíza" project by Herzog & de Meuron, 2009	Initiative financed by the Natal City Government Not yet completed
2015	Mãe Luíza Stairway	Rua Guanabara Constructed after the tragic collapse of the hillside on Guanabara Street that buried houses. The stairway finally provided direct access to the beaches.	Implemented by the Natal City Government with federal funds
2019	Houses for families displaced by the landslide	Rua João XXIII (next to the 4th Precinct)	Scheduled start of construction: December 2019, not yet started as of the publication of this book. Financed by the Federal Government

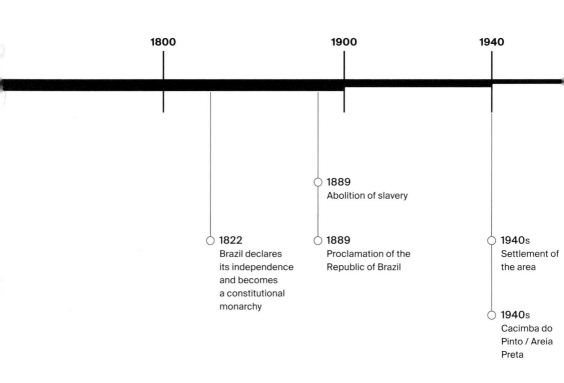

1800

1900

1940

○ 1889
Abolition of slavery

○ 1822
Brazil declares
its independence
and becomes
a constitutional
monarchy

○ 1889
Proclamation of the
Republic of Brazil

○ 1940s
Settlement of
the area

○ 1940s
Cacimba do
Pinto / Areia
Preta

Timeline

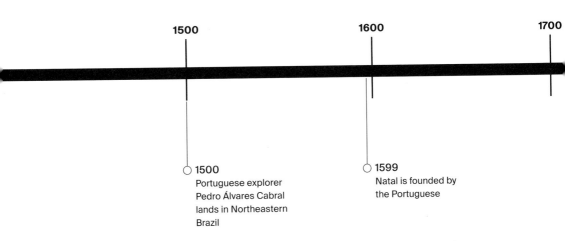

1500

1600

1700

○ **1500**
Portuguese explorer
Pedro Álvares Cabral
lands in Northeastern
Brazil

○ **1599**
Natal is founded by
the Portuguese

Brazil

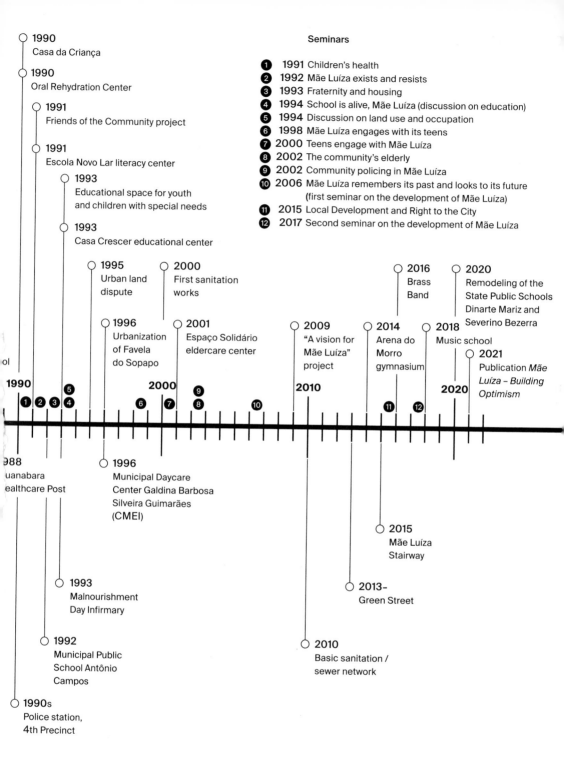

1990 Casa da Criança

1990 Oral Rehydration Center

1991 Friends of the Community project

1991 Escola Novo Lar literacy center

1993 Educational space for youth and children with special needs

1993 Casa Crescer educational center

1995 Urban land dispute

2000 First sanitation works

2016 Brass Band

2020 Remodeling of the State Public Schools Dinarte Mariz and Severino Bezerra

1996 Urbanization of Favela do Sopapo

2001 Espaço Solidário eldercare center

2009 "A vision for Mãe Luíza" project

2014 Arena do Morro gymnasium

2018 Music school

2021 Publication *Mãe Luíza – Building Optimism*

Seminars

❶ **1991** Children's health
❷ **1992** Mãe Luíza exists and resists
❸ **1993** Fraternity and housing
❹ **1994** School is alive, Mãe Luíza (discussion on education)
❺ **1994** Discussion on land use and occupation
❻ **1998** Mãe Luíza engages with its teens
❼ **2000** Teens engage with Mãe Luíza
❽ **2002** The community's elderly
❾ **2002** Community policing in Mãe Luíza
❿ **2006** Mãe Luíza remembers its past and looks to its future (first seminar on the development of Mãe Luíza)
⓫ **2015** Local Development and Right to the City
⓬ **2017** Second seminar on the development of Mãe Luíza

1990

2000

2010

2020

ɔl

Ə88 uanabara ealthcare Post

1996 Municipal Daycare Center Galdina Barbosa Silveira Guimarães (CMEI)

2015 Mãe Luíza Stairway

2013– Green Street

1993 Malnourishment Day Infirmary

1992 Municipal Public School Antônio Campos

2010 Basic sanitation / sewer network

1990s Police station, 4th Precinct

iect

Centro Sócio Milestones

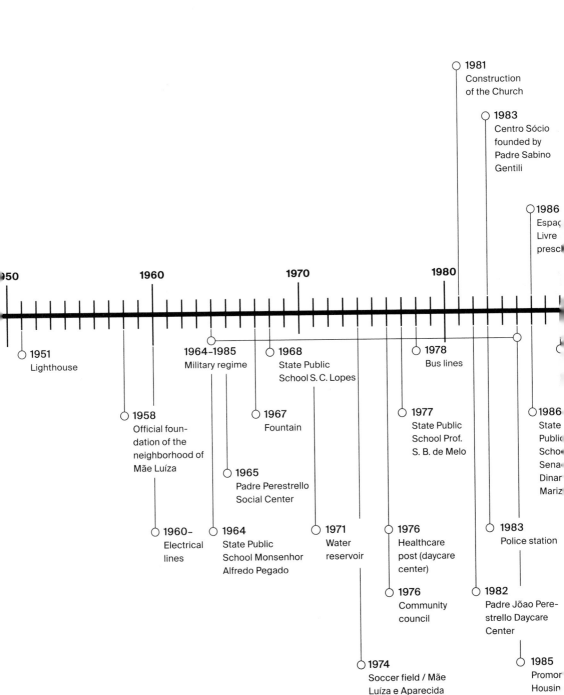

1981
Construction
of the Church

1983
Centro Sócio
founded by
Padre Sabino
Gentili

1986
Espaç
Livre
presc

1950   **1960**   **1970**   **1980**

1951
Lighthouse

1964–1985
Military regime

1968
State Public
School S. C. Lopes

1978
Bus lines

1958
Official foun-
dation of the
neighborhood of
Mãe Luíza

1967
Fountain

1977
State Public
School Prof.
S. B. de Melo

1986
State
Publi
Scho
Sena
Dinar
Mariz

1965
Padre Perestrello
Social Center

1960–
Electrical
lines

1964
State Public
School Monsenhor
Alfredo Pegado

1971
Water
reservoir

1976
Healthcare
post (daycare
center)

1983
Police station

1976
Community
council

1982
Padre Jõao Pere-
strello Daycare
Center

1974
Soccer field / Mãe
Luíza e Aparecida
sports center

1985
Promor
Housin

Mãe Luíza Public Milestones

Today's Green Street and Rua João XXIII, ca. 1980

Green Street and Rua João XXIII, ca. 2019

Mãe Luíza viewed from the dunes, ca. 1980

Mãe Luíza viewed from the dunes, 2020

118

Landslide area, 2015

Mãe Luíza Stairway at the site of the landslide, 2018

Rua João XXIII as seen from the Centro Sócio, 1987

Rua João XXIII as seen from the Centro Sócio, 2020

View of the old gymnasium from the Lighthouse, 2012

View of the newly completed Arena do Morro gymnasium from the Lighthouse, 2014

The old gymnasium, 2012

Arena do Morro gymnasium, 2020

122

1987

1981

Architectural Plans: Michel Cachat
Area: 300 m²
ca. 1,250 visitors monthly
Staff: 4
(2019)

Nossa Senhora da Conceição Catholic church

The church provides space to the Catholics of Mãe Luíza (about 60% of the neighborhood's residents). The parish offers religious services and is active in social activities for the entire community.

1983

ca. 1,000 visitors monthly
Staff: 4
(2019)

Centro Sócio Pastoral Nossa Senhora da Conceição, known simply as Centro Sócio

The Centro Sócio is the main building where residents can go to obtain general information, help and support. It is the link that connects the people in the community to all activities taking place in Mãe Luíza (see Historical Milestones, p. 106). Additionally, it is the administrative center for all projects. The Centro Sócio also houses a small museum and library as well as several rooms that can be used for other community activities.

1998

2019

124

2007

1986

Architect (initial building):
Heitor Andrade
Area: 460 m²
Students: 177 total
(91 female, 86 male)
Student age: 3–5 years
Staff: 11
(2019)

Espaço Livre preschool

The Espaço Livre preschool is an educational facility whose
instruction follows the public education curriculum. First
established at the Centro Sócio in 1986, a separate building
was erected in 1993. In 2018, one floor was added to the building,
which has since housed the Music School. The preschool still
occupies the ground floor.

2018

Preschool courtyard, 2018

126

1997

1993

Architects: Vinícius Pessoa Albino
and Heitor Andrade
Area: 591 m²
Students: 166 total
(71 female, 95 male)
Student age: 7–15 years
Staff: 17
(2019)

Casa Crescer educational center

Founded in 1993 as a school for children and adolescents,
Casa Crescer was, from the start, a provider of support, offering
craft workshops focused on generating income, and daily
meals to the poorest families. Today the Casa Crescer focuses
on educational support, and tutoring, and offers supplementary
meals to children in need.

2007

Casa Crescer (the large white house surrounded by school buildings) seen from the Lighthouse, 2012

2002

2001

Architect: Heitor Andrade
Area: 610 m²
Residents: 23
37 daycare participants
(Monday–Friday)
Staff: 33
(2019)

Espaço Solidário eldercare center

Established in 2001, the Espaço Solidário is today a point
of reference in the Mãe Luíza neighborhood as a home for the
elderly. People turn to it when an elderly person or family
member is in difficulty. Besides housing permanent residents,
it offers daycare services to the elderly population.

2019

2019

Alameda Padre Sabino Gentili before the Green Street project, 2008

130

2013

Urban Vision: Herzog & de Meuron
Urban Project: SEMURB, Carlos
Eduardo da Hora, Ana Karla Galvão,
Daniel Nicolau, Karenine Dantas
Projected length: 940 m
Completed: 540 meters of sidewalks,
70 meters of new pavement
Streetlamps: none are electrified

Green Street (Alameda Padre Sabino Gentili)

This project began in 2013, based on Herzog & de Meuron's urban planning proposal, "A Vision for Mãe Luíza," published in 2009. Thanks to the efforts of the Centro Sócio, the Natal City Government agreed to finance and implement the project. Its purpose is to offer the community a place for family leisure, community fellowship, and relaxation in the shade, among the trees and flowers. The Natal City Government has not yet completed the project, which has been stalled for years. For their part, residents have begun to plant and care for the trees and flowers.

Green Street at Centro Sócio, 2019

Green Street, individual plant pots, 2019

132

2014

Architects: Herzog & de Meuron
Area: 1,964 m^2
ca. 1,200 weekly users
Staff: 7
(2019)

Arena do Morro gymnasium

Situated across the street from the Lighthouse, the gymnasium has been open to the public since 2014. Built as a sports venue with the intention of welcoming many other activities, today besides sports, it houses cultural and festive events, concerts, workshops and gatherings and has become an intergenerational social center in Mãe Luíza.

Chess play in the multipurpose room, 2015

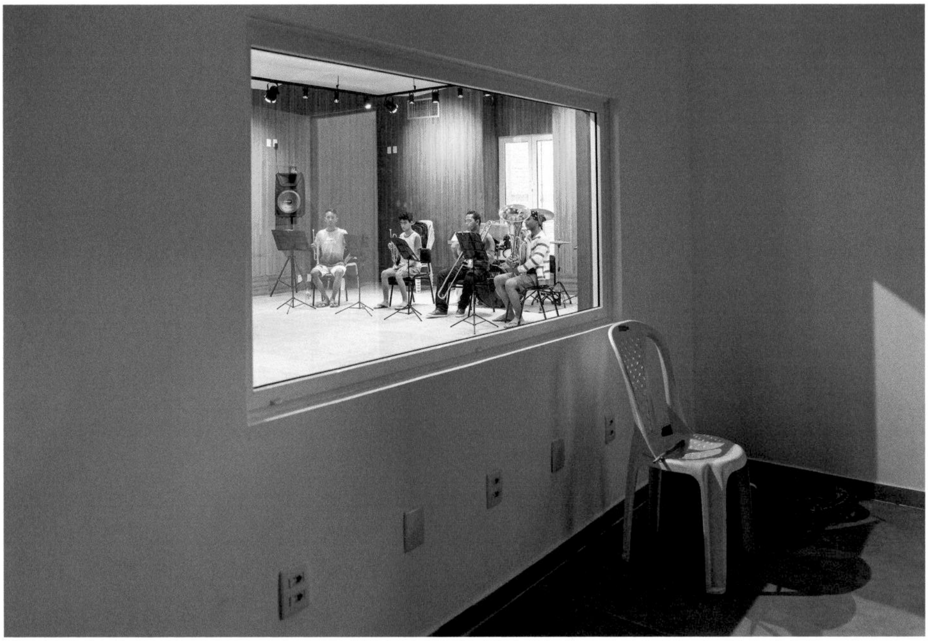

134

Rehearsal in the main hall, 2018

2016

35 members on average
Indefinite membership for graduates
of the Music School

Brass Band

The Brass Band is regularly invited to play for presentations and public events as well as in the traditional music Festival Mãestro Felinto Lúcio. As of 2021, the band has performed more than 100 times, including appearances with the Rio Grande do Norte State Symphony Orchestra.

2018

Architects: Kenya and
Eduardo Grunauer
Area: 253 m^2
Duration of education: 3 years
Students: 75 (about gender balanced)
Student age: 7–17 years
Teaching staff: 3
(2019)

Espaço Livre Music School

The Music School offers an education on wind and percussion instruments, reflecting the traditional music of Rio Grande do Norte. It provides all equipment and all instruments. Each instrument is shared by 2–3 students. Every student must pass an entry exam after a couple of months of solfege. Three students have already been accepted to the Technical School of Music of the Federal University of Rio Grande do Norte. With the enrollment of 25 students twice per year, the school seeks to train 1,000 musicians over the next 20 years.

Concert at the Music School, 2018

Ion de Andrade and Nicole Miescher

Padre Sabino Gentili

Born in Italy in 1945, Padre Sabino Gentili gave himself one mission: helping people. Thanks to his spirit of solidarity and his immense wisdom and culture, he carried out important work in Brazil: the establishment of the Centro Sócio in Mãe Luíza, the great engine behind the community's development.

136

Sabino Gentili was born July 13, 1945, in Castel di Tora, a small rural community about 80 km northeast of Rome, Italy. His family of subsistence farmers was poor. Sabino was an intelligent and interested student who was given to reading and reflection. At that time, the poor had access to education only through the Church. At age 11, Sabino Gentili left home to study with the Salesian Congregation in Rome. In 1972, he left Italy for Germany to complete his studies with the Salesians. Working in civil construction during school vacations gave him his first contact with the world of work and foreign cultures.

In 1973, Padre Sabino Gentili left for Brazil to become director of a traditional private Catholic school in Natal: the São José Salesian High School. In 1979, he gave up his post at the school and decided to serve the poor. He moved to Mãe Luíza and lived a life like that of his poor neighbors. Padre Sabino ended his career as parochial vicar of the neighborhood, one of the poorest in the city.

Padre Sabino was extremely learned. In addition to his mother tongue, Italian, he spoke Portuguese, German, French, Spanish, English and Latin. He was a tireless reader of the theology of all religions, from Judaism to Buddhism and including the African religions, and both Catholic and non-Catholic religious sought him out to discuss the most difficult problems they faced in relations with their communities and their faithful.

To this community of religious friends, he was considered not only a priest, but a man of God, with whom they felt at home and trusted. His ideals and attitudes were profoundly humanist.

Aside from his erudition, Padre Sabino was also passionate about popular culture. He knew all the soap operas and best-sellers and provided an impressive array of knowledgeable opinions.

No one understood how he found time for such things since, besides his religious life, he personally handled everything related to the Centro Sócio. Established by him on December 8, 1983, the Centro Sócio provided vital services to Mãe Luíza and came to represent the basis of the community's development.

The remarkable Padre Sabino was warm and generous. An unforgettable figure, he had wide-ranging and unorthodox ideas. He held a deep desire for a better and more just world, and he committed his life to realizing that dream with all his being and strength. He deeply believed in love and solidarity.

He was the driver of profound change in the life of Mãe Luíza's poor, helping build not only material improvements, but also the self-confidence needed for change and a pride in accomplishments. His life conveyed the message that dreams are not merely illusions, and that when we dream together, dreams can come true.

Padre Sabino devoted 29 years of his life to the Mãe Luíza community. He died July 8, 2006, of heart failure, a condition for which he had been treated for years. The disease that took him could not have better represented the way he was: his heart was too big.

The Centro Sócio is the work of this rare and simple man, great and humble, universal and loved, strong and sweet, religious and secular, European and Brazilian. Thanks to the Centro Sócio, the focus on the dignity of individuals and the community – an ideology to which Padre Sabino was always faithful – lives on in Mãe Luíza.

Sabino Gentili (1945–2006)

2006

Team Centro Sócio, 2006

Ion de Andrade

Struggles for Life and Survival

Wattle-and-daub houses, illiteracy, lack of water and electricity, and streets of sand – the fight against the prevailing precarious conditions in Mãe Luíza gained force and strength in the 1980s with the presence of the dedicated Padre Sabino and the Centro Sócio.

140

During the 1980s, the Mãe Luíza neighborhood found itself in a situation of extreme poverty. In November 1985, the minimum wage corresponded to about USD 60 per month. A look at the neighborhood's development timeline (see p. 111) reveals an urban structure that had received few improvements, and access to those was not universal. Included was a water reservoir, electricity, some schools, and a health unit put in place between 1960 and the late 1970s. The main streets of Mãe Luíza were paved with cobblestones, but secondary streets for the most part remained unpaved sand.

Although most houses already had running water, supply was irregular and often with low pressure, as it is even today, forcing families to store water in artisanal barrels, usually uncovered. This practice was inevitable in houses without running water.

Despite the availability of electricity, not everyone had access to it, and many houses were still lit by oil lamps. Understandably, not having electricity also implied inaccessibility to basic household appliances such as refrigerators to preserve quality and extend the shelf-life of food. Safe food storage not only allows cost savings, but also protects the family health. In most house-holds, food was cooked over a wood-fire since families could not afford to buy gas.

Houses were often built of wattle and daub and typically had earthen floors, which made cleaning difficult – even more precarious was the cardboard or straw used as building material in the Favela do Sopapo. Not all houses had bathrooms, a situation that resulted in families' burying excrement or placing it in the household trash for collection. The improper handling of waste and its always insufficient collection would often lead to an infestation of rats that would invade houses at night, attacking people.

In this scenario, infant mortality was high, and illiteracy was wide-spread.

This is the neighborhood where, in the early 1980s, Padre Sabino built a Catholic church and established the Centro Sócio, "the insti-tutional base," as he used to say, designed to offer the community the backing and credibility of the Church as it faced its struggles.

Through this dialogue, the community and the Centro Sócio built a roadmap of responses to the enormous challenges posed by survival.

The initial struggles focused on confronting what the community deemed its highest priorities. Such survey of needs guided the institution's activities, with initiatives driven by Community Seminars where problems and potential solutions were put forward for discussion by the community itself with the help of experts invited to take part.

Active in this scenario of real and generalized problems, the Centro Sócio strived to fulfill a priority agenda for the people. It established the Espaço Livre preschool (see Historical Milestones, p. 106). It also organized the first-ever neighborhood rat extermination, pressuring the city to fulfill its role in the process in which the community activity participated. With the Friends of the Community project, it developed a response to infant mortality. Through a community effort with residents, the Centro Sócio urbanized the Favela do Sopapo (cardboard and straw houses, no water, electricity, or sanitation), giving rise to the Brisa do Mar Housing Project, through an effort that also included the participation of professors from the Department of Architecture at UFRN.

In addition, guided by the Friends of the Community project, the Centro Sócio worked to improve the structure of several earthen floor houses that lacked bathrooms, and opened a malnourishment day infirmary for severely malnourished babies and an oral rehydration center for dehydrated babies, as well as sponsored the purchase of food for families in extreme poverty, actions viewed as synergistic in the fight against infant mortality.

The Casa Crescer educational center, founded in 1993 (see Historical Milestones, p. 107) additionally included establishment of a crafts workshop focused on generating income, and installation of a kitchen where the community's poorest families could get their main meal of the day.

This phase in the struggle for survival did not end abruptly, however. Several elements arose to indicate the emergence of a new stage, making it a transition from a "struggle for life and survival,"

142

to a "struggle for development and social inclusion." Two initiatives were discontinued, and two new projects were begun:

The Friends of the Community project was discontinued in 2001 since infant mortality as a result of preventable and treatable diseases appeared to have been overcome, and the Community Health Agents Program (owned by municipality) had been implemented in the neighborhood.

As a result of recording data on infant and general mortality, visiting mothers under the Friends of the Community project began to raise increasingly more issues related to aging. This resulted in the 2001 opening of the Espaço Solidário eldercare center (see Historical Milestones, p. 107). Former visitors under the Friends of the Community project were hired as caregivers to the elderly.

The Escola Novo Lar literacy center, an adult literacy school, ended up closing after the need for its services waned due to the increase in literacy levels, but in its place, the Computer Technology School opened its doors after the community held a seminar to discuss employability of its teens (see Historical Milestones, pp. 106–107).

The establishment of these spaces – the Espaço Solidário eldercare center, as a successor to the Friends of the Community project, and the Computer Technology School in the place of the Escola Novo Lar literacy center – is emblematic of the emergence of a new phase resulting from Mãe Luíza's struggles and collective efforts. In each of these initiatives, the government was all but absent.

Construction of Brisa do Mar Housing Project in place of the Favela
do Sopapo, 1996

Brisa do Mar Housing Project, 2012

Brisa do Mar Housing Project, 2008

Ion de Andrade

Infant Mortality

The Friends of the Community project was one of Centro Sócio's most impactful initiatives of the 1990s. Thanks to this project and its plan for continuing education, women in the community became "visiting mothers" and drastically reduced infant mortality rates in Mãe Luíza.

In the late 1980s and early 1990s, infant mortality amounted to 60–70% deaths per 1,000 live births in Mãe Luíza. With annual births averaging 350, this meant some 20–25 deaths per year. In the words of Padre Sabino Gentili, "two weeks didn't go by without the bells tolling for a baby." As is often the case with high infant mortality, most causes of death were avoidable and treatable: diarrhea, pneumonia, and malnutrition.

Hence, in 1991, the Centro Sócio organized a seminar on infant health that focused on illness prevention and the importance of breastfeeding and timely immunization. The community voiced concern about its lack of running water and electricity, factors that hindered safe food storage and increased the risk of diarrhea associated with water-quality issues. Many homes were found to not even have a toilet, forcing residents to bury excrement in their yards or place it in the household trash for collection.

For decades, advertising campaigns had undermined the practice of breastfeeding by claiming that powdered milk was better for babies. As a result, many women would breastfeed for a much shorter period than the recommended first six months, when a baby's diet can consist only of breast milk. With early weaning encouraged, families in poverty found themselves struggling to purchase enough powdered milk to ensure good infant nutrition, often leading to chronic malnutrition.

At the close of the seminar, the Centro Sócio proposed an initiative that would engage the community itself. Under the Friends of the Community project, ten mothers from the neighborhood of Mãe Luíza were assigned to pay monthly visits to all pregnant women and babies under the age of one. These visiting mothers were trained in the topics to be addressed during their rounds, including breastfeeding and early weaning; infant nutrition during the first year of life; diarrhea and dehydration; pneumonia and other respiratory illnesses; vaccination; malnutrition; prenatal care; and nutrition for pregnant women. This work was accompanied by an ongoing agenda in continuing education. Within two years, the neighborhood's infant mortality rate had dropped to around 15 deaths per 1,000 births.

As part of the project, cases were presented at weekly meetings and the group discussed the most challenging situations, such as serious disease, mental illness, violence, and extreme poverty, so that specific measures could be taken in each case. Members of the group did in-depth analyses of cases of infant death to sharpen the team's ability to detect life-threatening risks. As an outcome of these meetings, the Centro Sócio opened the Malnourishment Day Infirmary (see p. 141, Struggles for Life and Survival).

If visiting mothers identified a home that lacked bathrooms or a hard floor, the Centro Sócio provided sacks of cement. Families pitched in to help with construction, sometimes joined by volunteer architects. Each year, the visiting mothers recorded data on infant and general mortality. As a result, the project soon realized that the neighborhood population was aging.

After the Community Health Agents Program was implemented and infant mortality had declined noticeably, the Friends of the Community project was discontinued in 2001.

1995

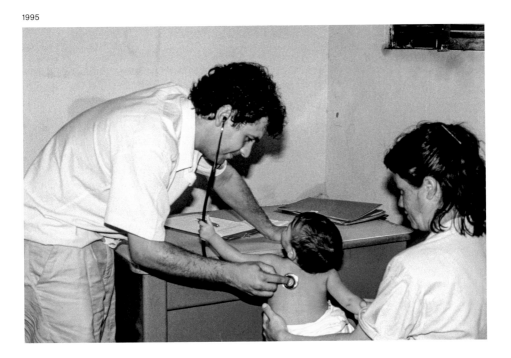

Ion de Andrade

Homicides in Mãe Luíza

The over 30-year commitment of the Centro Sócio in Mãe Luíza and its impact on the neighborhood's homicide rates is discussed. A comparative analysis of violence in Natal and Mãe Luíza brings several surprises from 2013–2019.

152

The work developed in Mãe Luíza during more than 30 years of dialogue between the Centro Sócio and the community can of course be expected to have had an impact on some of the key indicators of quality of life for the people living in the areas where the work was conducted.

Specifically, we should expect these indicators to have improved more in Mãe Luíza than elsewhere in the city. This means that if a given statistic showed improvement in Natal, and if an initiative with a bearing on this statistic was undertaken in Mãe Luíza, the corresponding indicator should perform better in this neighborhood. This is what happened with infant mortality in the 1990s, for example.

The performance of these indicators should reflect the efficacy of the work. This was also the case with the homicide rate, which has fallen faster in the neighborhood of Mãe Luíza than in the city of Natal overall. Since 2019, the homicide rate for Mãe Luíza, traditionally a violent place, has been lower than the rate for Natal.

The broken line in Graph 1 indicates the neighborhood's population as a percentage of the population of Natal, while the curved line shows homicides in Mãe Luíza as a percentage of homicides in Natal, from 2013 to 2019:

The rate of violence in Mãe Luíza was more than twice that of Natal's in 2013, accounting for 4.07% of all homicides (first point on the curve in the graph) but less than 2% of the total population (broken line). Note also that violence trended steadily downward from 2013 to 2016, with an especially sharp drop-off in 2015. This period witnessed no new public initiatives in the neighborhood, other than the April 2014 opening of the Arena do Morro gymnasium. Yet the number of homicides kept falling. Given how often families with young people who were in positions of social vulnerability asked us to invite these youth to take part in activities at the new facility, it is indeed tempting to attribute this to the new gym.

This decrease in the number of homicides is particularly noteworthy since Natal was classified among the world's 20 most violent cities in 2016. One of the many reports to this affect published at that time was a *Deutsche Welle Brasil* article dated January 26, 2016, which ranked Natal as the world's 13th most violent city (https://www.dw.com/pt-br/brasil-tem-21-das-50-cidades-mais-violentas-do-mundo/a-19005124). The same finding was registered in a Forbes article from August 31, 2016 (https://forbes.com.br/listas/2016/08/20-cidades-mais-violentas-mundo/). According to international indicators, this held true until late 2018, when the city was no longer cited among the world's most violent. Throughout this timeframe, homicides continued to decline in Mãe Luíza.

During this period of darkness for the city of Natal, it should be expected that homicides would have skyrocketed in Mãe Luíza, a community suffering the effects of social exclusion, inequality, and entrenched violence. Yet surprisingly, the neighborhood trended in the opposite direction, with violence decreasing there while it rose in Natal overall.

Complementing the previous graph, Graph 2 shows that the number of homicides per 100,000 inhabitants likewise fell, despite all forecasts to the contrary and against a backdrop of adversities. By the end of the decade, the homicide rate in Mãe Luíza was lower than that of the city's overall.

Note that the curve indicating homicides per 100,000 inhabitants is flatter for Natal than for Mãe Luíza, with murders per 100,000 inhabitants in fact increasing from 63 to 68 for 2013–2017. The rate for Natal only begins to decline in 2018. Conversely, the curve for Mãe Luíza dips downward almost steadily from 2013 to 2019, except for a slight upswing in 2016.

These results demonstrate that Mãe Luíza stood out from the rest of Natal over this six-year period. Graph 1, which plots the homicide rate in Mãe Luíza as a percentage of homicides in Natal, indicates that the neighborhood became proportionately less violent in 2019. This is consonant with the data found in Graph 2, which illustrates that the homicide rate per 100,000 inhabitants in Mãe Luíza dropped below that of the city overall for the first time during this period in 2019.

These data suggest that the initiatives implemented in Mãe Luíza were quite effective in reducing homicides, criminality, and violence in the neighborhood.

1 Source: Annual reports of the Observatório da Violência (OBVIO) and the Instituto Brasileiro de Geografia e Estatística (IBGE)

2 Source: Annual reports of the Observatório da Violência (OBVIO)

53

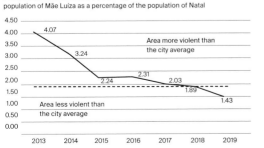

1 Homicides in Mãe Luíza as a percentage of homicides in Natal and the population of Mãe Luíza as a percentage of the population of Natal

- - - Population of Mãe Luíza as a percentage of the population of Natal
— Homicides in Mãe Luíza as a percentage of homicides in Natal

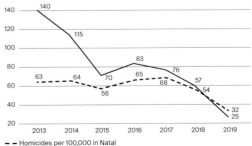

2 Homicides per 100,000 inhabitants in Mãe Luíza and Natal

- - Homicides per 100,000 in Natal
— Homicides per 100,000 in Mãe Luíza

Ion de Andrade

Struggle for Development and Social Inclusion

Once the struggle for survival as a primary goal was over, the Centro Sócio and the community began to call for a development model for social inclusion. Important improvements were achieved, the most impactful and transformative among them being the Arena do Morro gymnasium, built in 2014.

Around 2004, after various thematic seminars focused on the difficulties faced in Mãe Luíza, it was becoming clear to the Centro Sócio council that all these problems stemmed from a larger underlying problem, a kind of chronic underdevelopment resulting from the weak presence of government in the community's daily life, which produced continuous social exclusion. It was then realized that there were really three interrelated problems: the neglectful state, chronic underdevelopment, and social exclusion.

It is interesting to note that it took 20 years for the Centro Sócio to arrive at an analysis that was to some extent obvious. The major difficulty of identifying the main component of this social exclusion was the result of something that continues to be a cause of the other components: the neglectful government, noticeable precisely because of its passivity or absence.

When the government does make its presence felt in Brazil's poor neighborhoods, it limits itself to opening school networks and basic health units, facilities whose universality are legally obligatory. Nothing else is mandatory. This means any action that goes beyond what is strictly required under the law depends on pressure from citizens or the goodwill of city managers. To make matters worse, conventional wisdom has always tended to blame the excluded for their own exclusion, thus exempting the government from any responsibility.

If schools do not operate and there are not enough teachers, it is because people do not organize in order to exert pressure. If the streets are not lit, it is people's fault for not having mobilized to demand it. Thus, what would never be demanded of those from the privileged sectors is demanded of the poor, who must obtain through their own struggles everything the wealthy have by dint of birth.

In 2006, the Centro Sócio organized a community seminar to discuss development, entitled "Mãe Luíza Remembers its History and Plans its Future." For the first time, ideas that were not just related to survival surfaced. The community noted the lack of space devoted to sports, leisure, and culture, expressed its concerns about employment and mobility, reflected on its urban beauty, and pointed out that the community did not have a single funeral home.

Yet by the close of the 2006 seminar, the Centro Sócio, despite its extensive experience, still had not comprehended the vast qualitative difference between the new agenda and the previous one, and as always, sought only to fulfill the ideas expressed in that seminar.

It was the Ameropa Foundation that proposed implementation of one of the seminar's initiatives – the one involving sports – because of its potential to reach a large number of people, particularly young people, while still opening its doors to other age groups. Added to that is the notion that sports involves self-discipline, teamwork, rules, victories, and defeats, all of which are fundamental virtues for young people.

The 2014 opening of the Arena do Morro gymnasium gave shape to the most important achievement to come out of the 2006 seminar. It made it clear to the Centro Sócio council that the institution, working together with the community, had built a development model for social inclusion based on (a) social participation and (b) implementation of public policies and local social structures, in response to the difficulties faced by the community.

This achievement made it even more clear that government had not taken a leading role in facing and resolving those issues and that the Mãe Luíza community had only achieved a response as a result of its own mobilization. Moreover, this had only been possible because of the unlikely presence of an institution endowed with a participatory work methodology and a network of international supporters.

Only after the opening of the gymnasium did the Centro Sócio realize that the struggles in Mãe Luíza had gone through two historical stages: survival and development of social inclusion (a phase that had its first expression in the gymnasium). And it finally understood that this second phase gave value and meaning to the struggles for survival.

These discoveries encouraged the Centro Sócio to share its experiences as a way to make the Mãe Luíza's unprecedented roadmap of responses available to the urban peripheries and rural areas of the state of Rio Grande do Norte and Brazil.

Then the Centro Sócio invited the city's social and community movements to take part in the Seminar "Local Development and the Right to the City," which drafted the 2015 Natal Charter for social movements.

We highlight below some of the achievements in Mãe Luíza from 2015–2020 related to this new approach to the struggles for development and social inclusion that began to guide the community's aspirations and demands, in some cases, beyond the action of the Centro Sócio:

– Green Street (initiated in 2009, but still incomplete due to inaction by the Natal City Goverment – the installed light poles were not electrified and only 70 meters of the 940-meter project have been newly paved)
– Renovation of Edgar Borges Square, which added a stage for performances (2013);
– The Mãe Luíza Stairway connecting Avenida Guanabara to the oceanside Via Costeira road, built on the site of the mudslide that destroyed Avenida Guanabara (2015);
– Reorganization of the Surf School, including providing it with a head office, using funds from the nearby Areia Preta Neighborhood Association (2019);
– The Brass Band, composed of 35 young musicians, established in 2016;
– The Music School belonging to the Centro Sócio, opened in 2018;
– The 2020 renovation and expansion of State Public Schools Senador Dinarte Mariz and Prof. Severino Bezerra de Melo as a result of intense mobilization by the Centro Sócio council to create synergy between the gymnasium and neighborhood schools.

The Mãe Luíza Stairway, 2018

The Banda filarmónica de Cruzeta in concert at the Arena do Morro, 2016

The women's group Flores de Jacaranda performs regularly at the Espaço Solidário, 2020

Mass at the church, 2020

Evening shopping, 2018

Celebrating 25 years of Casa Crescer, 2018

Preschool pick-up, 2019

Art class on the terrace of Arena do Morro gymnasium, 2020

Green Street, event area, 2016

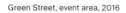

Verner Monteiro

Urban Conditions in Mãe Luíza

A Comparative Analysis in Statistics Data and Maps for the Decade 2009–2019

This chapter is intended to compare general urban statistics from the last decade for the city of Natal and the neighborhood of Mãe Luíza. These statistics are mainly related to infrastructure and urban services as particular aspects of urban living conditions in Mãe Luíza and the city, and therefore, reflect essentially public action or human geography. The most recent data available was collected between 2017 and 2019, and compared to statistics presented in the book, *A Vision for Mãe Luíza*, published in 2009. The statistics chosen to be briefly analyzed include density, income, water supply, sewage system and learning facilities. These five statistics were selected on the assumption that they are the most direct way to examine basic living conditions and their improvement over the decade up to 2019.

In conclusion, the present brief analysis of basic statistics indicates that Natal did not undergo considerable changes over the last decade, while Mãe Luíza substantially improved, in comparison. It raised income in real terms, improved sewage connections, and increased and upgraded its learning facilities. For the reviewed period, the neighborhood increased its population density by 13%. The only statistic to reveal a deterioration in conditions was the number of water connections since a substantial portion of them had been destroyed during the landslide of 2014. The renovations carried out in the schools were substantial, in part related to the perception of new levels of urban demand resulting from the presence of facilities like the Arena do Morro gymnasium in Mãe Luíza, suggesting that development produces a systemic response. The progress achieved by substantially increasing the number of new sewage connections introduces the potential for improvement of public health in the neighborhood.

Two architecture students from the Federal University of Rio Grande do Norte, Thales Lemos and Kelvin Johnson, worked under the supervision of Professor Verner Monteiro to complete this chapter. They gathered data from different sources, including city administration, the Brazilian Institute of Geography and Statistics, and the Federal University of Rio Grande do Norte, using it to illustrate the maps presented to facilitate visual comparison. The 2009 maps were developed by the Herzog & de Meuron team through a similar process.

Density

Density data is important because it shows how people are concentrated in the urban areas, indicating such things as the need for better infrastructure. The two comparative maps presented with this topic indicate that density consistently increased in three areas North of the Potengi River, which now makes them some of the densest parts of the city. The above-mentioned neighborhoods, along with Mãe Luíza, have very similar characteristics: poor urban conditions, such as low water supply, few sewage connections, and a high rate of garbage production. Mãe Luíza has increased its population density by 13% and has maintained a stable position as the most densely populated area in Natal.

Inhab. / ha
- 140–
- 100–140
- 60–100
- 40– 60
- 20– 40
- 0– 20

2009

Natal	51.27 [Inhab. / ha]
Mãe Luíza	175.40 [Inhab. / ha]

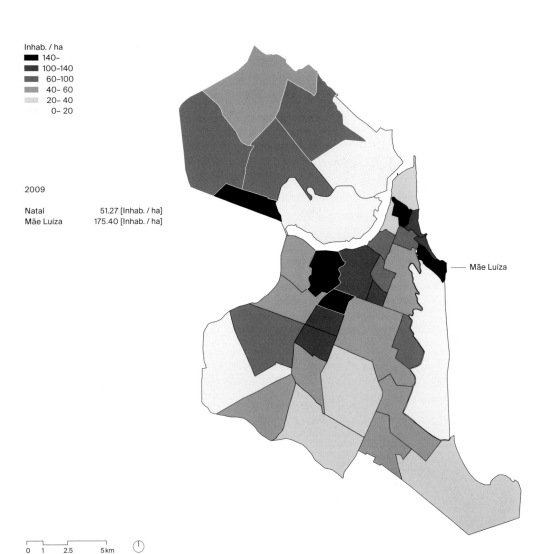

Mãe Luíza

0 1 2.5 5 km

2019

Natal   53.19 [Inhab. / ha]
Mãe Luíza   198.93 [Inhab. / ha]

Mãe Luíza

Income

Income reflects the financial independence of families, giving them the capacity to buy everyday goods, such as food and medicine. An income map can also indicate the city's concentration of wealth. Income comparisons of average salary (as multiplication of minimal wage) between maps show almost no difference for Natal for the decade after 2009. Some of the neighborhoods that were analyzed increased income slightly. These are in the eastern and southern parts of the city.

Considering that inflation for the period 2009–2019 was 77%, Mãe Luíza gained around 58% in purchasing power over the inflation rate, which suggests there were positive changes in family income.

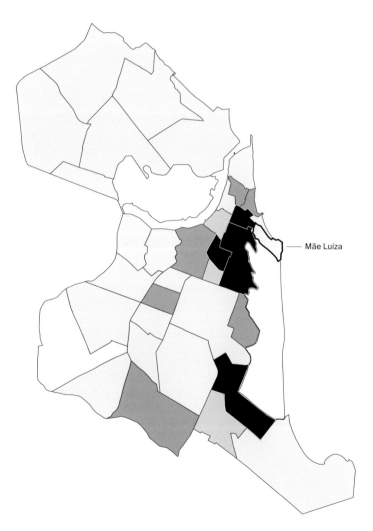

Average salary as multiplication of minimum wage*

- 11–15
- 5–11
- 6–8
- 4–6
- 2–4
- 0–2

*R$ 465 [R$ 1 = USD 0.57, 11/2009]

2009

Average income	[per month in R$]
Natal	919.10
Mãe Luíza	310.34
São Paulo	2,139.58
Brazil	1,143.34

Mãe Luíza

0   1   2.5   5 km

2019

Average income	[per month in R$]
Natal	1,776.44
Mãe Luíza	868.26
São Paulo	unknown
Brazil	unknown

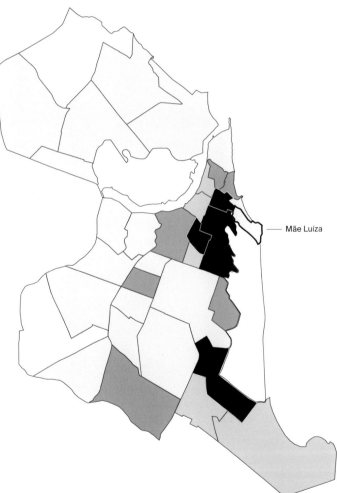

Mãe Luíza

Water Supply

Water supply is a basic infrastructure condition that directly impacts public health. Providing water to the population is important as it offers minimum conditions for cooking, washing, and drinking. Statistics from the last decade show that more homes are connected in both the southern and northern parts of Natal, and that Mãe Luíza apparently lost a third of its connections. This can be explained by the huge landslide of 2014, which damaged a large number of connections.

Water connections

- 12,000–
- 8,000–12,000
- 5,000– 8,000
- 3,000– 5,000
- 1,000– 3,000
- 0– 1,000

● contaminated areas

2009

Water connections [general network]
Natal   172,815
Mãe Luíza   3,691

Mãe Luíza

0 1   2.5   5 km

It may also be that authorities had overestimated the number of
water connections before the landslide given the difficulty involved
in accessing all buildings due to security concerns, and had
no precise data. The detailed survey of water connections after
the landslide shows the actual condition of the infrastructure.

2019

Water connections [general network]
Natal   201,930
Mãe Luíza   2,768

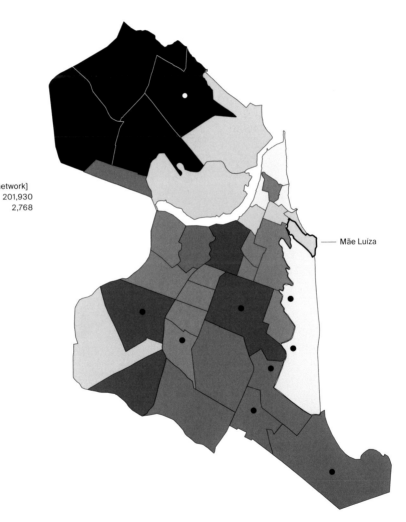

—— Mãe Luíza

Sewage System

Along with water supply, sewage systems are of key importance for ensuring good public health conditions. A good system prevents the propagation of numerous infectious diseases, such as diarrhea. With regard to sewage systems, the benefits of the decade up to 2019 mainly appeared in the central neighborhoods that have better income and economic conditions. However, two changes in the poor areas are notable: one of the northern neighborhoods had a consistent increase in sewage connections and Mãe Luíza benefited from a more than twofold increase in the number of sewage connections per home, reaching the status of where almost half of all neighborhood properties are connected.

Sewage connections

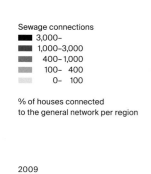

- 3,000–
- 1,000–3,000
- 400–1,000
- 100– 400
- 0– 100

% of houses connected
to the general network per region

2009

Sewage connections [general network]
Natal   45,261
Mãe Luíza   791

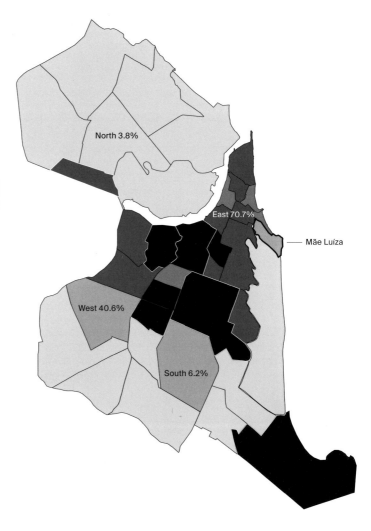

North 3.8%

East 70.7%

Mãe Luíza

West 40.6%

South 6.2%

0   1   2.5   5 km

2019

Sewage connections [general network]
Natal   71,892
Mãe Luíza   1,794

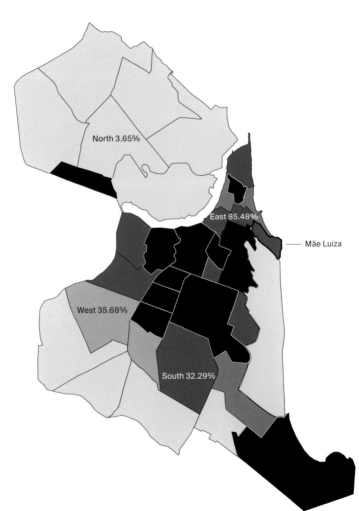

North 3.65%

East 85.48%

Mãe Luíza

West 35.68%

South 32.29%

Learning Facilities

Education can make a substantial difference to people's futures, especially in developing countries. One of the ways to check a city's current educational status is by mapping the number and distribution of learning facilities. Natal presented almost no change during the decade considered. Several private universities were established as a result of a policy to democratize access to higher education on the part of low-income groups in Brazil through a partnership between the federal government and the private education sector.

Universities
○ private
◉ public

Schools
• preschool
● municipal-state
⬤ federal

2009

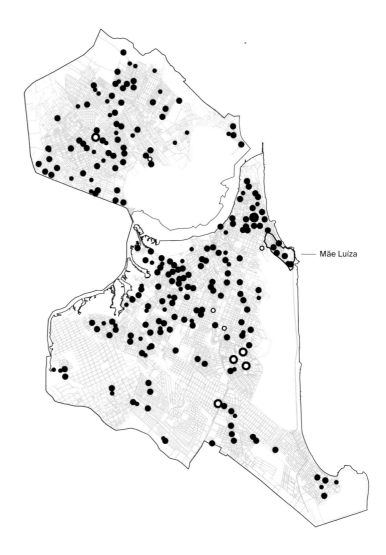

Mãe Luíza

0   1   2.5   5 km

Mãe Luíza gained two preschools, raising the number of public schools from six to eight during the period. The State Public School Senador Dinarte Mariz, where the Arena do Morro is built, has been substantially enlarged and remodeled, and the State Public School Prof. Severino Bezerra de Melo has been renovated in 2020.

2019

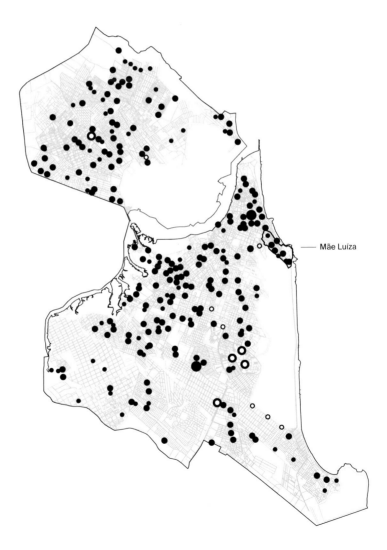

Mãe Luíza

Dulce Bentes

The Mãe Luíza Law
Fight for Land, Resistance, and Challenges to the Law

Two decades of struggle gave birth to Law no. 4.663 of 1995, the document
that guaranteed the right to live in the neighborhood of Mãe Luíza in the 1990s.
This piece discusses what has changed since then, and the challenges of
ensuring social housing.

On their road to obtaining land rights, residents of Mãe Luíza won
passage of a piece of legislation central to guaranteeing their
permanence in the neighborhood: Law no. 4.663 of 1995, which
recognized Mãe Luíza as a "Special Area of Social Interest" (*Zona
Especial de Interesse Social*) within the City of Natal Master Plan.
The prime purpose of this land tenure instrument is to create and
maintain social housing by recognizing the rights of informal settlements and minimizing gentrification. We know that no law in and
of itself has the power to produce transformations or bring about the
inclusion of populations historically invisible to public policy. However, laws that are born through the struggles of excluded populations often become valuable instruments in the conquest of rights.

In the 1970s and 1980s, the residents of Mãe Luíza watched as
the city tore down their homes, an event that took place in informal
settlements across Brazil. The ensuing struggle for housing
rights unfolded in a political context of re-emergent social movements, as part of the fight to return Brazil to democracy. A social
movement took root in Mãe Luíza in opposition to the implementation of large real estate ventures there.

In the early 1980s, Parque das Dunas State Park was created
along the Via Costeira roadway, bringing pressure to do away with
residential occupation in Mãe Luíza. In the early 1990s, three
by-the-hour motels were built on land along Avenida João XXIII,
near Via Costeira. These facilities basically served short-stay
clients and were not part of the plans for the Via Costeira Hotel
District. Because Mãe Luíza is located near this tourist area,
the community was affected by these activities and the situation
became a topic for discussion.

In 1992, a hotel project called Paradiso Mare Resort was put forward,
including plans to build on the site of a protected dune formation,
next to the Mãe Luíza Lighthouse. This further mobilized community groups committed to defending the neighborhood.

Aside from their environmental impact, these large tourist facilities
were expected to have evident social impacts and to affect land
prices. Since rising real estate costs could push local populations
out of the area and back to underserved, peripheral areas, this
was a critical matter.

The community seminar "Mãe Luíza exists and resists," held in 1992, played a major role in underscoring the threat of gentrification as the neighborhood grew. Representatives of public agencies, NGOs, and teaching and research institutions were invited to help with discussions. In the Environmental Group of which I was part, researchers from various fields examined how these large projects might impact the neighborhood and indicated how land-use planning needed to be compatible with Mãe Luíza's specific social and environmental situation. It was concluded that the urban planning instruments and specifications stipulated in the 1984 City of Natal Master Plan, then in effect, would not guarantee social and environmental protections for the neighborhood. Although Mãe Luíza was incorporated into this plan as a Special Area of Urban Recovery, a specific law that took local characteristics into account was needed. These efforts were spearheaded by resident representatives, under the leadership of Padre Sabino of the Centro Sócio, and technical assistance was provided by students and faculty from the Architecture and Urban Planning course at the Federal University of Rio Grande do Norte. The urban plan was completed in 1992 and approved by the municipal legislature on July 31, 1995, in the form of Law no. 4.663.

Grounded in socioeconomic, cultural, and environmental considerations, the Mãe Luíza Law promoted a variety of urban activities. Lot size may not exceed 200 m^2, which has historically been the neighborhood's average size and which exceeds the minimum area of 125 m^2 defined for residential housing under federal legislation. This requirement represents an important, strategic mechanism for discouraging large real estate ventures and gentrification.

Furthermore, the definition of a two-story maximum is consonant with area infrastructure and the fact that the neighborhood lies on a range of sand dunes now part of the Parque das Dunas. These requirements will guide neighborhood development by reconciling urban expansion with social and economic inclusion and with cultural and environmental protection. In the 25 years since enactment of the Mãe Luíza Law, new institutions, businesses, and services have opened, local supermarkets have gained firmer footing, and other social facilities have been built, for example, the Arena do Morro gymnasium, wholly designed and licensed pursuant to the legal codes of the Mãe Luíza Special Area of Social Interest.

The Arena do Morro gymnasium proves that a large public building can be constructed in compliance with norms. It is also clear that when the community secured passage of this legal instrument and thus guaranteed land access, it strengthened social projects and facilities that had been achieved through earlier struggles, while likewise fortifying resistance in the face of both land conflicts and numerous attempts to change or eliminate the rights provided for in the law.

The City of Natal Master Plan is now up for review, however, and the proposals currently on the table suggest that ground may be lost in the realm of protective measures for "Special Areas of Social Interest." Without the social and environmental protection mechanisms defined under the Mãe Luíza Law, residents may well find it very difficult to remain in the neighborhood and enjoy the benefits of urbanization won through their struggles.

The weakening of these rights has driven up property values, taxes, and water and electricity rates. While gentrification has not been a regular part of neighborhood development, islands of high-priced housing may eventually appear inside areas of popular housing. This means it is essential to maintain and reinforce the social and environmental rights defined under the Mãe Luíza Law so that present and future generations can remain there and so that the neighborhood is preserved as an asset built through collective struggle and action.

Projected site of Paradiso Mare Resort, 1992

Start of tower construction along the coastline, 2006

Full wall of coastal towers between Mãe Luíza and the ocean, 2019

Ion de Andrade

Institutional Principles

Long-term planning, synergy among organizations, community participation, joint initiatives, and management transparency shape the scope of the Centro Sócio and offer the institution recognition and credibility in the struggle for development and social inclusion.

The Centro Sócio has continued to serve as a catalyst in the process of development toward social inclusion in Mãe Luíza. But what is a catalyst? In chemistry, a catalyst is a substance that increases the speed of a chemical reaction without being consumed in the process. What then do we mean by "development?"

This is an important question because the institution eventually realized that the problems faced by the Mãe Luíza community over the course of more than 30 years were always linked to a single underlying issue: the oppressive presence of chronic underdevelopment resulting from the continued absence of government and its abnegation of responsibility in the face of the community's tangible problems. So when we talk about "development," we are referring to a process of overcoming social exclusion. It is in going from this notion of development toward social inclusion that the Centro Sócio has been and continues to be a catalyst.

Padre Sabino's idea for establishing the Centro Sócio was, in his own words, to "create a platform that could use the credibility of the Catholic Church to help the community in its institutional organization and struggles." The institution had within itself the values and organizational principles that led it to play a role that was neither expected nor given a priori, and this is an important part of its innovative and extraordinary character, not just in that neighborhood, but also at the national level.

One significant feature of that character is the fact that the Centro Sócio – as a secular institution connected to the Catholic Church – is prepared for long-term work, like that of the Church. This time-management perspective gave the institution the ability to plant without major concern for the timing of the harvest. A good example of this was the 2006 seminar that discussed the neighborhood's development and that was still bearing fruit in 2018 with the opening of the Music School.

A second and equally important feature emerged from Padre Sabino's positioning of the Centro Sócio as an institution at the service of the community's organization and struggles, thereby creating an institution whose work was in service to others and not to itself. It was not up to the Centro Sócio to establish the agenda, but rather to support and foster the process of reflection within the community, lending it an institutional platform. For this reason, the institution never made unilateral decisions. Instead, initiatives were always implemented after community seminars, where problems were spelled out and possible solutions identified.

The Centro Sócio has always been responsible for systematizing the proposals drafted by residents and carrying out the projects together with the community. Each of the institutional spaces – the Espaço Livre preschool and the Music School, the Casa Crescer educational center, and the Espaço Solidário eldercare center – has always had important moments when it listened closely to its collectivity in order to make decisions. In this way, the Centro Sócio had always functioned as an interpreter of the collective will expressed through several participative activities.

That role gave the institution credibility and recognition that today go beyond the boundaries of Mãe Luíza. The Centro Sócio has become a respected liaison, facilitating institutional dialogue with the executive (state and municipal) and legislative branches, although it does not ensure that their demands are met.

In times of crisis, like the present, resulting from the COVID-19 pandemic – as well as when the Avenida Guanabara mudslide left dozens homeless – the community turns to Centro Sócio, recognizing it always as the institution that receives and distributes donations that come into Mãe Luíza. This is only possible because the nature of its work is disinterested in any kind of benefit, power, or prestige on behalf of the institution itself, allowing it to be guided only by the agenda that is subjectively more important for the community.

All of this has been materially possible solely because the institution could count on the material and continuous support of other institutions that understood the need for long-term construction over the course of these many years. The Ameropa Foundation, the Association of Friends of Mãe Luíza of Switzerland, the Penzberg Parish, the Women's Community Mülhausen and the Brazil Aid Eggenthal have been partners of the Centro Sócio for decades. The most significant government support came into play five years ago when it granted Centro Sócio exemption from payment of social security charges, a legal right of philanthropic institutions.

The local government contributes small sums to the Espaço Livre preschool and the Espaço Solidário eldercare center.

The institution has always valued continuing education for its employees in addition to its meticulous accounting management and expenditure planning. The council has remained stable throughout this period, a fact that has allowed it to adhere to the same methodological approach needed for three decades, always prioritizing listening in order to interpret the community's expressed will.

The Centro Sócio currently has 68 employees, not to mention the work of volunteers and interns from several educational institutions. In a neighborhood with nearly 15,000 inhabitants, the Centro Sócio sees more than 1,000 people every month through its direct services at the institution's headquarters. Every day it receives 418 students among the three schools (literacy, educational support, and music), and nearly 60 elderly, both residents and those in daycare at the Espaço Solidário. Through 2019, approximately 4,800 people have been welcomed to various activities at the Arena do Morro gymnasium.

For 30 years, the institution has used a methodology of constant listening to put together a roadmap of responses to a very precarious reality that has been transformed over time. Subsequent analysis of that roadmap has allowed us to identify two major historical phases in terms of organization and community struggle: the first phase focuses on confronting survival and the second phase prioritizes fostering development and building social inclusion.

Loyse de Andrade

Mãe Luíza's Aging Population

Over 20 years of working with the elderly, the Espaço Solidário has welcomed residents or hosted elderly in the daycare center around the practices developed by all stakeholders.

The aging of Mãe Luíza's residents has gone hand in hand with the increase in Brazil's elderly population. Today, adults over the age of 60 represent approximately 10% of the neighborhood's inhabitants.

In recent years, the elderly have been guaranteed social security and constitutional rights by law primarily through Brazil's Statute of the Elderly. This is a considerable step forward because the Statute of the Elderly determines the obligations towards vulnerable elderly, placing the onus first on family and then on the State. But the law was not accompanied by policies capable of helping the most vulnerable families who were unable to support their elderly members, nor did it implement other alternatives for providing shelter to the elderly without social support, confirming the precariousness of the assistance.

It is worth noting that most Long-Term Residential Institutions for the Elderly (ILPIs) in Brazil are private non-profit organizations. In Brazil's Northeast, these house 81% of the elderly residents in institutions. The other 19% are housed in private for-profit institutions, designed for a higher income clientele. In the state of Rio Grande do Norte, less than 0.5% of the elderly are housed in ILPIs, which reveals the enormous scope of repressed demand. The city of Natal, with 884,000 inhabitants, has only 240 spaces for elderly without social support.

After ten years of work through the Friends of the Community project involving maternal-infant care, Mãe Luíza saw a decline in infant mortality rates and the emergence of the new problem of population aging. Daily contact with the families began to reveal some disturbing situations: homeless elderly and physically and cognitively impaired or totally helpless elderly living alone. These are recurring circumstances that are discussed at weekly meetings with the health team from the Centro Sócio. The anguish when faced with the lack of support alternatives able to improve the situation of these elderly began to represent a new challenge for the Centro Sócio.

In 2001, the Espaço Solidário eldercare center was established (see Historical Milestones, p. 107 and Fact Sheet, p. 128). From that time, the center has sought to be a place of continuous learning for both the elderly and team members alike.

The facility developed its practices with the elderly through weekly meetings, creating a place for listening and building a daily life capable of involving them in a dynamic and participatory process that affirmed their dignity and whatever autonomy remained them. The facility's team meets biweekly to discuss issues and study the aging process to improve and revise its practices as needed. This process of collective construction involves the community, family members, and friends, who are always invited to share in the care with us as well as to take part in activities such as parties and be present in the discussions. In fact, what makes the Espaço Solidário so special is its management structure involving the elderly, the community, the team and the family and friends of those under its care.

Over the course of 19 years, the center has housed nearly 80 elderly residents and hosted more than 150 elderly in the daycare center. Residents spend an average of eight years at our facility – a considerable amount of time (in Switzerland, for example, the average is three years), which indicates a quality of life capable of extending longevity.

Despite constant concern over the sustainability of the Espaço Solidário, the facility's presence for the past 19 years has profoundly altered neighborhood life and shown that it is possible to improve the reality of aging in Brazil's low-income communities.

Mass at Espaço Solidário, 2020

Ion de Andrade

Natal Charter

Conceived by the Centro Sócio and revolving around three concepts, aimed at local development of the poorest communities, the embodiment of citizenship, and the implementation of strategic social facilities, the Natal Charter is a powerful tool that gave the capital's poorest groups a public presence and reaffirmed the Right to the City.

Local Development and the Right to the City

Released on March 28, 2015, the Natal Charter is a document written by social and community movements in Natal, Rio Grande do Norte, at the invitation of the Centro Sócio. The Charter encourages a strategic partnership between communities, especially low-income ones, and government for the purpose of achieving local development. The design of the Arena do Morro gymnasium and the experience of shared community management of the facility served as inspiration for the document.

While Brazil has made progress at a material level since the 2000s, the Charter points to the lack of any significant change in relations between the State and communities. Local initiatives are still limited to investments in a few uncertain projects, which include schools, daycare centers, healthcare facilities, and policing. The Charter in fact urges a deep shift in government-community relations, opening the way for a consistent public presence in the realms of sports, leisure, culture, urbanism, and elder care, accompanied by a commitment to the overall dignity of community residents.

The Charter revolves around three concepts:
– Local development aimed at improving quality of life and achieving community emancipation, grounded in the operationalization of an integrated public policy agenda that will sustain the continued presence of government in these communities.
– The Right to the City, a process by which citizens stake claim to an increasingly accessible, safe, and friendly city that affords universal access to culture, sports, and leisure.
– Strategic social facilities, defined as a set of social facilities that can generate community opportunities in myriad areas.

By incorporating these concepts, communities will have access to such social facilities as libraries, theaters, pedestrian walkways, multisport gyms, public swimming pools, cultural centers, elder living facilities, and funeral homes. The absence of these facilities makes life challenging, unstable, and distressful.

The Charter's main pillars are:
– Local participatory planning, access to the city, and strategic social facilities.
– Public funding of projects.
– Shared government-community management of strategic social facilities.
– Social control of public policy and budgets.

With these main pillars in mind, the Charter offers communities and government a series of recommendations and suggestions that will allow the proposed model to be replicated elsewhere.

Conceived in Mãe Luíza, one of Natal's poorest neighborhoods, the Charter invites Brazil to embrace a new model of social victories, one that ensures human dignity and citizenship.

Ion de Andrade

The Inclusion Network

Derived from the Natal Charter, this document proposes a new city experience for periphery and rural areas of Brazil, in the name of universal access to social inclusion and public policies with the support of sustainable budget planning.

Five years after the Natal Charter (see page 192) was released, the endeavor still had achieved only minimal practical results, although it had attracted much attention among urban planners. Hopes had been high that similar experiences might take root outside Mãe Luíza, but this was not the case. Only a few scattered initiatives in Natal drew inspiration from the ideas contained in the Charter.

We realized this might be partly due to the Charter's failure to include studies establishing how the related costs might impact public budgets. We also recognized that because the Charter had been released in a non-election year, opportunities had been missed to secure greater government commitment, which often comes only through public programs prepared before elections.

We reached the conclusion that the Natal Charter had failed to delineate the institutional bases essential to undertaking these initiatives. The Charter was a fine idea, but it needed to consider practical matters as well.

We then launched a study to ascertain how the Charter could become a more efficacious tool. A group of people from the Centro Sócio and the fields of architecture, sociology, and management was invited to participate. The discussions produced a tool called the Inclusion Network and Right to the City, or Inclusion Network for short.

As an outgrowth of the Natal Charter, the Inclusion Network is meant to demonstrate that it is indeed feasible to provide residents of Brazil's urban peripheries and rural areas with ongoing access to inclusive public policies and collective sports, cultural, and leisure facilities. The Network serves to operationalize a different experience of the city for people living there, one that fosters emancipation and dignity. The document uses the concept "periphery" not just in a geographic sense but to encompass vulnerable populations in general.

Depending on their specific needs, communities may adopt any of the gamut of initiatives suggested by the Inclusion Network, ranging from public swimming pools to daycare centers for the elderly and from environmental safety measures to cultural spaces.

State capital	Population	Poorest one-third (policy target)	Poorest one-third per 20,000 inhabitants	Proposed cost per municipality, based on BRL 1.5 million per 20,000 inhabitants per annum	Effective municipal budget (2019/2020)	Proposed percent of municipal budget
Porto Velho	442,701	147,567	7	BRL 11,067,525	BRL 1,558,036,080	0.71%
Rio Branco	348,354	116,118	6	BRL 8,708,850	BRL 829,051,331	1.05%
Manaus	1,861,838	620,613	31	BRL 46,545,950	BRL 5,149,837,000	0.90%
Boa Vista	296,959	98,986	5	BRL 7,423,975	BRL 1,344,914,737	0.55%
Belém	1,410,430	470,143	24	BRL 35,260,750	BRL 3,725,147,000	0.95%
Macapá	415,554	138,518	7	BRL 10,388,850	BRL 840,068,000	1.24%
Palmas	242,070	80,690	4	BRL 6,051,750	BRL 1,364,000,000	0.44%
São Luís	1,039,610	346,537	17	BRL 25,990,250	BRL 3,390,370,000	0.77%
Teresina	830,231	276,744	14	BRL 20,755,775	BRL 3,590,015,000	0.58%
Fortaleza	2,500,194	833,398	42	BRL 62,504,850	BRL 8,541,489,019	0.73%
Natal	817,590	272,530	14	BRL 20,439,750	BRL 3,226,694,000	0.63%
João Pessoa	742,478	247,493	12	BRL 18,561,950	BRL 2,322,071,000	0.80%
Recife	1,555,039	518,346	26	BRL 38,875,975	BRL 6,375,627,000	0.61%
Maceió	953,393	317,798	16	BRL 23,834,825	BRL 2,600,000,000	0.92%
Aracaju	587,701	195,900	10	BRL 14,692,525	BRL 2,382,000,000	0.62%
Salvador	2,710,968	903,656	45	BRL 67,774,200	BRL 8,022,875,000	0.84%
Belo Horizonte	2,395,785	798,595	40	BRL 59,894,625	BRL 12,106,581,000	0.49%
Vitória	333,162	111,054	6	BRL 8,329,050	BRL 1,659,981,077	0.50%
Rio de Janeiro	6,390,290	2,130,097	107	BRL 159,757,250	BRL 31,001,430,204	0.52%
São Paulo	11,376,685	3,792,228	190	BRL 284,417,125	BRL 65,662,001,878	0.43%
Curitiba	1,776,761	592,254	30	BRL 44,419,025	BRL 9,400,000,000	0.47%
Florianópolis	433,158	144,386	7	BRL 10,828,950	BRL 2,048,266,161	0.53%
Porto Alegre	1,416,714	472,238	24	BRL 35,417,850	BRL 7,723,000,000	0.46%
Campo Grande	805,397	268,466	13	BRL 20,134,925	BRL 4,307,329,000	0.47%
Cuiabá	561,329	187,110	9	BRL 14,033,225	BRL 2,663,916,427	0.53%
Goiânia	1,333,767	444,589	22	BRL 33,344,175	BRL 5,756,298,170	0.58%
Total	46,226,690	15,408,897	770	BRL 1,155,667,250	BRL 197,590,999,084	0.58%

The table shows the methodology for obtaining the budgets needed to materialize the Inclusion Network for each state capital in Brazil and how much this represents of the total municipal budget.

Communities should play a lead decision-making role in the planning of these initiatives, policies, and collective facilities.

Drafted not just with Natal but with all Brazil in mind, the Inclusion Network project defined the population to be targeted by these policies as the poorest 30% and calculated expected costs as a percentage of budgets for each state capital in Brazil. The study showed that the entire agenda of initiatives could be implemented by investing between 0.5% and 1.0% of the budgets of the state capital cities or 0.2% of federal budgets.

The study also estimated costs of staff, maintenance, and administration. Findings demonstrated the initiative's feasibility, especially if all three levels of government (federal, state, and local) take part in funding.

The Inclusion Network believes that development problems can be solved and social inclusion achieved by fostering community involvement. The Network should be operationalized by targeting government funds to the priority issues identified by each community.

The document ends with four commitments that candidates running for mayor or council member should pledge to implement:
– At least 0.5%–1% of the municipal budget will be allocated, organically and definitively, to the Inclusion Network's agenda of infrastructural and public policy proposals to ensure the project's sustainability as a government policy.
– Investments will be guided by participatory territorial planning for the short, medium, and long terms, with each community involved in designing its own local development project.
– Pursuant to participatory methodology, each community will be given a list of potential proposals that indicate what can be done within available budgets, because it is hard to dream and fight for what is unknown or seems unachievable when you have been excluded socially.
– This collective initiative will be prioritized by the municipality and will be actualized as public policy.

The ideals of the Inclusion Network lie within Brazil's grasp, and implementation of Network projects would help greatly improve the current situation.

Padre Robério Camilo da Silva

The Strength of Belonging in the Mãe Luíza Neighborhood

Identity in Mãe Luíza is linked to sharing both the precariousness as well as the joy of the last 30+ years of struggle for survival and social inclusion. With the presence of the Centro Sócio, residents also achieved pride in the neighborhood's achievements as they reflect on the spirit of belonging.

A feeling of identity has been extraordinarily strong in Mãe Luíza ever since its first residents arrived in the 1940s. Drought and economic pressure made it impossible for many people to remain in their communities, prompting a wave of rural exodus in the 1950s, with families leaving the countryside and moving to the peripheries of big cities. The result was the emergence of urban favelas.

So it was that people arriving from various corners of the state built their homes atop a lovely dune overlooking the sea. Identity ties gradually formed on the basis of shared needs, first housing and then the struggle for food, water, and work. People survived and were able to remain in this new territory because they managed to satisfy their basic needs at a minimum level.

We should bear in mind that these homes were made of straw, wattle and daub, cardboard, and wood, longstanding features of informal settlements and favelas in Brazil. They had neither water nor electricity. There was no birth control, so families were large and forced to live in small houses. Since there was no basic sanitation, many children died. Although living conditions were extremely precarious, it did not keep more people from leaving the countryside in hopes of a better life.

As the community grew, so too did the social problems typical of favelas back then, and these were no longer invisible to the government. Political authorities had to turn their attention to the sizeable population living atop the beautiful dune formation. On January 23, 1958, the community officially became the neighborhood of Mãe Luíza. This recognition bolstered residents' sense of identity and pride in belonging to Mãe Luíza. They secured many improvements through their demands and actions.

One element has always played a vital role in cementing this sense of identity: the memories recounted by the community's earliest residents and older members. Parents share their stories with their children; grandparents, with their grandchildren. These recollections are greatly respected, for they are often accompanied by tears. They are accounts of resilience, heroism, and much struggle, narrated as examples of honesty and incentive for today's youth, who so often find themselves without direction. What really matters is that the elderly are not ashamed of their past; rather, they are proud of it – they are winners. The fruits of their mighty battles are their homes, built with great sacrifice; their children, educated and employed; and the fact that they have remained in their neighborhood, against all odds.

After the Centro Social was established in 1983 by the beloved Padre Sabino, the community was encouraged to substitute the notion of identity with reflection on a sense of belonging. At the time, the neighborhood had a population of roughly 15,000 and incomes rarely exceeded USD 60 a month (in 2020 the minimum wage was R$ 1045, corresponding to around USD 180–200).

The Centro Sócio became a major ally in a series of struggles to improve the standard of living. The first and most urgent of these was the battle to reduce the neighborhood's extremely high infant mortality rates by providing support and protection to hungry, and therefore ailing, children. Many lives were saved as a result. Later, in 1993, the Casa Crescer educational center was established (see Historical Milestones, p. 107), providing the type of age-level appropriate intervention that is essential to steering youth away from drug addiction and potential crime.

A sense of belonging manifests itself strongly during moments of collective suffering, whenever the community feels threatened. Through discussions and organization, Mãe Luíza began to understand its identity as it worked to build solutions using the collective approach adopted at the Centro Sócio. But it is more than that. This sense of belonging, borne of pain and struggles, has enabled the community of Mãe Luíza to establish a robust approach to finding solutions for its problems. Answers are not seen as coming from the outside, but as generated within the community itself, whether these solutions are government-supported, as with the reform and expansion of schools, or whether the assistance comes from the outside, from sponsoring institutions such as the Ameropa Foundation and the Swiss firm of Herzog & de Meuron, which have helped support the Arena do Morro gymnasium and the Music School.

This sense of belonging evinces itself in the community's tremendous respect for these physical spaces, which have not, for example, become the target of the graffiti so commonplace in many neighborhoods. Truly embraced as public community spaces, these locations have also been free of theft.

Recognizing this intuitively, the Centro Sócio has made collective management of all its spaces a central value. Monthly meetings are held with parents and family members at schools, at the Espaço Solidário eldercare center, and also at the Arena do Morro gymnasium, with its Management Committee. The community has constructed itself and developed its own public spaces through this dialogue.

All this should serve as a model for public management throughout Brazil.

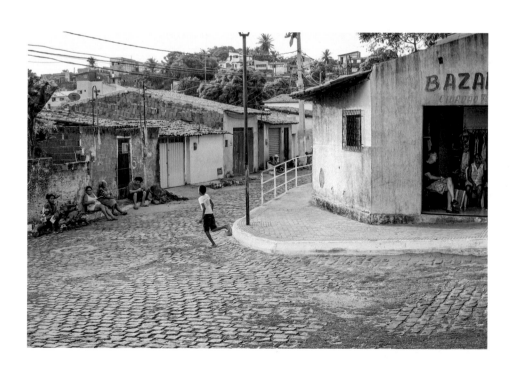

Strassenmarkt, 2018

Padre Robério Camilo da Silva, Ion de Andrade, Loyse de Andrade,
Edilsa Gadelha, Nicole Miescher, Josélia Silva dos Santos

What Has and Has Not Changed

This piece offers a summary of the progress achieved in Mãe Luíza after three decades of work. It has gone from a "non-neighborhood" of wattle-and-daub houses, no lights or running water to one with access to piped water, electricity, education, health, recreation, houses, and renewed hope. The changes identified are symbols of solidarity and point to what remains to be changed.

What has changed in Mãe Luíza

Positive Changes

– Reduction in infant mortality preceding Brazil's general reduction starting in 2000.
– Reduction in malnutrition during the first year of life due to greater adherence to breastfeeding. This occurred before Brazil's general reduction in malnutrition starting in 2004.
– As of 2004, construction materials for houses improved. Wattle and daub and fragile construction materials were almost entirely replaced by masonry.
– As of 2004, access to running water, electricity, and sanitation improved, and from about 2010, houses started to be renovated and painted.
– Improvements to sidewalks.
– Improvement in waste collection.
– Reduction of rat infestation.
– The original sand streets were paved or covered with cobblestones.
– Flowers and trees were planted in the streets by residents as well as the municipality.
– Illiteracy decreased among young people and adults, and the number of students accepted to universities increased.
– Renovation of two state schools out of a total of 41 schools renovated in Rio Grande do Norte.
– Emergence of bars and small restaurants enhancing the neighborhood's social life.
– The favelas, viewed as precarious settlements, no longer exist.
– Improved transportation.
– Visibly more cars belonging to residents.
  Better, although still precarious, basic community healthcare.

– Better care for the elderly, mainly due to the Espaço Solidário eldercare center.
– Lower levels of violence and a drop in homicides, now proportionally less numerous than in Natal.
– Opportunities for sports, music and cultural activities.
– A palpable change in mentality, strengthening the sense of identity and community, as well as greater self-confidence, especially among the young.

Negative Changes

– Presence of highrises in front of Mãe Luíza, cutting down on ventilation, access and views.
– Danger of gentrification by the real estate business in Natal.

What has not changed in Mãe Luíza

– Unemployment and scarcity of formal jobs. There is virtually no skilled employment.
– The government rarely acts in the interest of the community unless pressured to do so.
– Natal's perception of Mãe Luíza remains negative.

Many things changed and much was achieved during the last 30 years. There is still much left to be done.

Erminia Maricato

Mãe Luíza – Report from a Visit in July 2018

How do you build inclusive territories? That question is answered in a visit to the contradictory and fascinating universe of Mãe Luíza.

In late July 2018, I went to Natal to speak at the opening of the seminar "Caminhos para a construção de territórios inclusivos" (Pathways to the building of inclusive territories). The event was organized by the Federal University of Rio Grande do Norte, in conjunction with the Archdiocese of Natal and the NGOs Observatório Social do Nordeste and Fórum do Direito à Cidade.

Some of the lessons we learned in Natal came from the Centro Sócio in the community of Mãe Luíza. While Mãe Luíza is something of an exception, it is not the only favela in Brazil that offers its residents a range of cultural and sports activities, in this case including a brass band whose music would delight any visitor. The setting for these activities is an architecturally unique space designed by the award-winning Swiss firm of Herzog & de Meuron. From planning through maintenance, the facility has been funded by a Swiss philanthropic foundation. It was Mãe Luíza's success with these cultural endeavors in sports and the arts that inspired many communities in the city to join in drawing up the Natal Charter.

The Natal Charter does not limit the demands of working men and women to matters of survival, such as housing and transportation or minimum needs in education and health. Rather, it proposes to fight for quality public facilities that will enable children and youth on the urban periphery to develop their full potential. The Natal Charter also calls for a return to the practice of participatory budgeting, which wisely seeks to take public funds out of the hands of powerful lobbies.

The real estate boom that hit Brazil in 2009–2016 had a highly predatory impact on Natal and other large- and medium-sized cities. With the city of Natal revising its Master Plan, a further threat is now posed to Mãe Luíza and other neighborhoods along the coastline. Extremely dense land use and intense verticalization have been accompanied by new forms of segregation and exclusion, with lower-income social strata pushed into housing projects scattered far from the urban center.

Despite all of this, residents in these communities are exercising their citizenship with contagious energy and are actively and creatively reengaging in the practice of direct democracy – vital to securing a new future.

Excerpted and adapted from "O desastre urbano e os despertares," *Outras Palavras*, published on August 7, 2018, available at https://outraspalavras.net/cidadesemtranse/o-desastre-urbano-e-os-despertares/

Jacques Herzog (JH), Ascan Mergenthaler (AM)
and Lars Müller (LM) in Conversation

Arena do Morro

After the year 2000, the social order in Mãe Luíza had established itself enough
to make thinking about expanding infrastructure possible. The idea was to express
the optimism that social developments had become robust and sustainable
enough to be reflected in the townscape, and that such interventions would
be used, appreciated and cultivated. Nicole Miescher of the Ameropa Foundation
was able to benefit from having architect friends in her native Basel. Herzog
& de Meuron is a world-renowned architectural office known for its site-specific
planning and projects. What follows is a conversation with the architects about
their project and their working methods.

LM Nicole always looks for a perspective from outside and
brings in experts for her projects. How did you proceed?
You weren't just commissioned to build a sports facility but also
to apply your expertise to intervention in the local fabric as a
whole. You conducted extensive research to familiarize yourself
with Brazil and Natal and then zoomed in on this small neighborhood of Mãe Luíza.

AM Actually, Nicole really did ask us, "How would you feel about
building a gymnasium, a sports facility, for Mãe Luíza?" We
realized that we couldn't just design and build a facility without
understanding the location itself, and so we replied, "Let's
study the location, do research, and get in touch with people at
universities, people who are familiar with the location, so that
we can start from there and gather information." The result was
a little book, *A Vision for Mãe Luíza,* an important document.
In addition to careful analysis of Natal and Mãe Luíza, it outlines
all of the basic building blocks: how city planning and architecture
might develop in this location over the next decades. You might
say, those are the guidelines that we defined and developed on the
basis of what we found there.

JH Pierre and I have known Nicole personally for almost 40 years.
We have always been in contact over the years and also done
buildings together. She is an interesting, extraordinarily open person. She also has an artistic streak. That's important in connection
with a project that is obviously not going to be commercial but
rather an adventure. We didn't want to be traditional about developing architectural projects at ETH Studio Basel (see p. 272). Instead
we studied cities and landscapes, especially areas and places
characterized by informal neighborhoods. Mãe Luíza is an informal
urban neighborhood of that kind. That poses a crucial question:
Does it make sense for an architect to intervene there? Of course
we can make reasonable suggestions but there's no telling how
they will be received and how people will live with them. And in the
case of the Arena [do Morro], only the future will tell, even though
it already seems to be a success. We want to find out whether it
makes sense to build – and if so, what –, whether building proposals
meet with acceptance and whether they will actually improve the

situation in the long term. Or whether the architecture we envision works only in our culture, our cities, which are not informally structured but governed by clear-cut rules and regulations.

LM You then came to the conclusion that intervention on your part could be meaningful and interesting. On one hand, there is the history of Mãe Luíza, the social givens, and on the other, the exotic look of the place as we perceive it. If you want to intervene and accentuate certain things, how do the social circumstances and aesthetic givens influence the task at hand? How did you come up with the Green Street? It is the backbone, as it were, an axis straight through the neighborhood in contrast to the pinpointed accent of the Arena. What was your answer to the specific conditions there?

M The answer came from studying how this place grew: informally, even though there were certain regulations. For example, here are astonishingly strict maximum heights and building ordinances that we have to comply with. That partially explains why there is a certain uniformity to what has been built. Of course, the details show a great deal of individuality because the people in Mãe Luíza love to give their houses a personal touch with lots of color and elaborate wrought iron grilles. So we looked very closely at the layout of the neighborhood and were struck pretty quickly by this double street, the Alameda Padre Sabino Gentili and Rua João XXIII. Why were there two streets here and not one? That led to the idea of confining motorized traffic to one street and turning the other into a "Green Street." Our recommendation read: "Turn it into a market, a street only for people, a meeting place, so that traffic doesn't ruin both streets." In addition, this axis redefined as a Green Street is geared towards the edges of the neighborhood where you can sense the natural environs and the ocean nearby. That yields a stringent framework, a backbone along which Mãe Luíza can continue to develop. This simple but effective suggestion was immediately embraced and exploited by the local residents. Over time, they built and extended the Green Street in keeping with their own expectations. A new planting piece is added every year, increasingly fleshing out the green axis. It is extremely gratifying to see how such a process need only be given initial impetus for it to take off and develop on its own.

JH People build informal settlements for their daily needs with their own ideas and their own potential – and not according to the ideas of outside planners or authorities. Public space belongs to the daily needs of people but is more challenging to design and structure because it requires communication, consensus and an organization that directs the process. So when we say: "make a green axis there for pedestrians and leave the other street to cars," that sounds good to us and I think it's reasonable, too. But how does it sound to the others and how can it be implemented without destroying the entire fabric? Ultimately the people themselves have to want it and make it happen. The right thing to do is probably observe developments and see how things pan out in practice. Step by step. Then there's a chance that it will work.

LM That sounds plausible. A society has to achieve a certain health in order to be receptive to interventions of that kind. And there also has to be a need for intervention. The timing was right in Mãe Luíza for both projects, for the Arena at the head as well as the Green Street as the backbone.

AM Nothing will grow if you sow seeds on dry earth. You have to prepare the field and irrigate it. This is exactly what the Centro Soçio, the Ameropa Foundation and the international network have been doing for over 30 years – the spadework for further development.

LM About the Arena: I remember a small drawing showing the rafters of the hall and the drawing continuing along the edge of the gable, enlarging the volume and opening it up to the street. Once again you can see how existing givens become a point of departure.

AM It was only a roof, not even a hall, just a roof. In fact, only the rafters of a roof. The idea of expanding the roof was presented with other possible scenarios and then selected and supported by the community.

LM You extended the roof and closed off the lot facing the street. I like the pragmatism, reacting to what's there: thinking about it and making drawings to move on from there. The Green Street was originally an ordinary street. Now it's green and upgraded by having a different function. You took the same approach to the Arena, by making an urban correction. The first time I approached it by car, I had the impression of something fortified, protective and defiant. When you climb up and reach the top, you feel like a prince standing in his tower…. lording it over the world below.

AM The two sides of the building are very different – that's important. The defiance, the slightly elevated feeling comes from the topography and by rigorously extruding the geometry of the existing roof structure over the entire site. That way the body of the building facing the ocean and the view acquires a certain height and thus an attitude, a look forward. In the direction of the neighborhood and the school, the building is very low, with a fine, human scale. The roof is so low you can touch it. The first idea – a large roof for everyone, extending over the entire property – was a good basis for the further development of the project.

LM The height and eye-level access are sensuously perceptible qualities of the building.

AM They are implicit qualities and it's important for the building to have both: it's not actually elevated facing the view but rather the building displays an attitude. At the same time, it's a wonderfully open, low-threshold building – a very inviting place.

JH There's something modest about it, even ordinary, that I really appreciate. Modest because it doesn't act monumental; it doesn't show off, you might say, despite the size of the area that it covers. It's also like a covered square, where sports and games already took place beforehand. The way it was constructed is ordinary: layers of single stones with ventilation slits of the kind you see everywhere in the south – like the structures people build for themselves in the favelas.

LM Thanks to overlapping uses, the Arena has a small-scale feeling that people really like. It is conspicuously asymmetrical. The rectangular playing field in the center has clear-cut rules of play while the periphery is broken up, divided into rounded shapes, open and permeable. To me, that's an architectural response to the informal and its aesthetic. I think that lowering the height of the school to human scale and opening the building towards the south permits a sensuous approach, symbolically linked, to my mind, with optimism – even if you didn't explicitly aim for that. By being open, permeable and nonauthoritarian, the Arena invites participation. The collective respect and use of the building by people who don't usually think about architecture shows that they have accepted the invitation and taken possession of the building.

AM I think it's not just the material but the building itself that makes for this openness. The inside is flooded with natural light and air, that's an important aspect. It really is only a roof with protective walls, see-through walls. You take part in what's happening on the opposite side. That really sets it apart from other gymnasiums that we visited in the area. There, no matter how bright the light is outside, you always walk into a dark hall, maybe with a skylight through which the sun shines down like a laser beam. The fact that we managed to break up the structure so that the entire space is flooded with natural light and air is what gives the building such quality. People really enjoy it because they don't walk into a hermetically sealed room that is cut off from the world outside. It's a public place that provides protection from the searing sun and the occasional rain. A place that was initially conceived for just sports has been opened up for other uses and activities. It's used for education, people make music there, and older people get together there as well. These uses are in addition to the sports because the building is flexible and inviting; it is not a monofunctional sports facility.

LM It is hard to play football in a concert hall. But you can listen to a concert or celebrate mass on a football field. It's impressive how well suited the Arena is for a concert or a town meeting despite its primary use as a sports arena. People appreciate the multipurpose use of the building even if they don't pay any attention to the architecture. Is there method to this aspect at Herzog & de Meuron? Has a tried-and-tested approach been adopted and applied to Mãe Luíza and Brazilian culture? You have essentially distilled the aesthetic canon of the location in the way that you incorporate the Arena into the urban fabric and deliberately use reduced, familiar materials.

JH No, we don't have a prescribed method. But we obviously look very closely at where we are and who we are working for. As mentioned at the beginning, our approach is similar to that of the ETH Studio Basel. Every place on this planet is different; it's about specific people with specific needs. After all, we want to improve a place; we want to make it more pleasant, more practical and more beautiful. Maybe more humane, too. That has always been a raison d'être of architecture. And that also applies here in this part of the world that is still relatively new to us. We used perforated brick walls for the shell of the building. People there are familiar with them. Ours are, of course, more carefully made. Yes, maybe care is a better term than beauty in this case. I think people sense that something has been made for them. For each of them individually as well as for the community. It's really gratifying to see how much people respect this new place. Even so, it's hard to make a prognosis, let alone any claims, as to how it will develop over the years. Whatever the case, we do think that beautiful and carefully conceived architecture makes a significant impact on how life unfolds in and around it.

AM Maybe it was initially thought of as a building for young people – also to give them a future. It is so gratifying that the use of the building now really spans generations. There is room there for everybody. The Arena is like a forum; it's an offer. Another word about the aesthetic canon of the location. We put a lot of thought into the colors – because Brazil is so colorful. One idea was to include color in the design of the building, but we rejected that idea and decided to use only the color of the materials themselves. Vibrant colors come from the users themselves. People in Brazil love color; their clothing and their colorful approach to life are simply marvelous. We didn't want to compete with that. That's why the building is so understated and that's exactly what makes it stand out in the neighborhood and in the entire town. It soaks up the colorful life there.

JH Color would certainly have been an option for Mãe Luíza – because everything is so colorful there. But "color and architecture" is a thorny issue. There are not many examples that have been able to endure. Besides, it would have been a particular challenge to work with color in Brazil because people do that all the time in their own homes. To suit their own taste. It's very personal and they often redo it, paint over it again, doors, window frames, inside walls, outside walls, railings – in bold colors and uninhibited combinations. You can't copy that; what they do is better, really vibrant. And getting an artist on board to work on a color scheme with us, which we have done occasionally, would have been inappropriate here.

LM It's good to see how people have intuitively accepted the Arena and how the new building is incorporated quite naturally into the aesthetics of the location. I often talk to Nicole about her search for beauty, her study of it. I think the aesthetic expression of the informal also defines the identity of the place. Beauty lies in the eye of the beholder. Your motivation in building the Arena is different from what motivates people to create an identity of their own and distinguish themselves from others, whether it's pink walls and green door frames or through clothing. The Arena has created a place that belongs to everybody; it has become part of their collective identity.

AM I'm not sure if the people in Mãe Luíza think the Arena do Morro is beautiful. Maybe it's more about the way they feel when they are in the building; it feels "beautiful" and light and good. They feel comfortable there and that attracts them. That's fantastic! It would be a completely different matter if they had built it themselves and maybe they would have also given it a bit of paint. But the whole trick lies in the neutrality of its appearance: the simple design of the roof, the quality of the light and the natural ventilation appeal to people's sense perception. That's beyond beauty. The Arena is a perception machine. It is cooler inside than outside, without the help of technology. The light is as bright

inside as it is outside, but it's pleasantly diffuse. That attracts
people to the arena, that's why they want to be there.

     JH I think it's a bit absurd for us to try to describe the beauty
     and aesthetics of this new place. It's not our job but rather
     that of architectural critics or outsiders to evaluate our archi-
     tecture. No matter what anybody says, it doesn't change anything.
     The only thing that counts is whether the architectural works
     in everyday life – and it's great that this seems to be succeeding
     in Mãe Luíza.

     Translated by Catherine Schelbert

The old gymnasium seen from the dunes, 2006

0 50 100   250 m

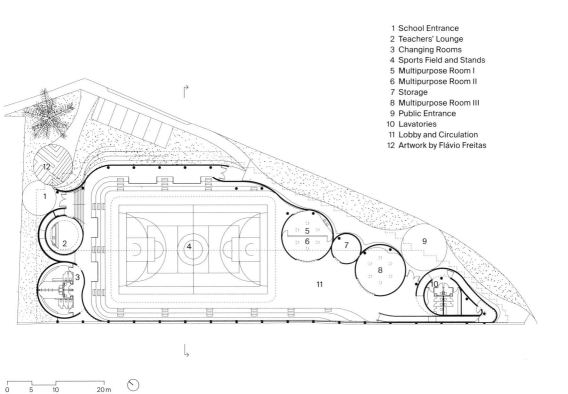

1 School Entrance
2 Teachers' Lounge
3 Changing Rooms
4 Sports Field and Stands
5 Multipurpose Room I
6 Multipurpose Room II
7 Storage
8 Multipurpose Room III
9 Public Entrance
10 Lavatories
11 Lobby and Circulation
12 Artwork by Flávio Freitas

0   5   10   20 m

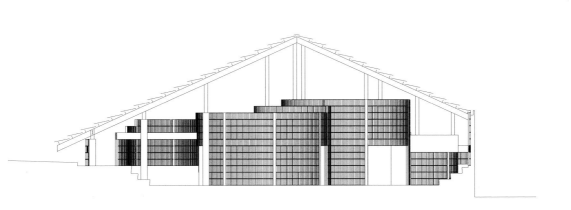

0   2.5   5   10 m

Raymund Ryan

Building Optimism: Mãe Luíza Rising

When joint construction is undertaken by outsiders but planned after properly listening to the community and considering the project's surroundings and ramifications, something fundamental is introduced: horizontal collaboration and a community spirit of transformation.

As the world turns, evolving in ways concurrently positive and negative, the relationship of privileged and underprivileged societies to each other is in constant flux. South America occupies a hybrid position in any too-easy First World/Third World dichotomy, exhibiting manifestations or symptoms of both, and mixing the physical evidence in unorthodox ways.

Back in the 1920s, Oswald de Andrade proposed the concept of Anthropophagism, a provocative idea that Brazilian culture essentially cannibalizes other cultures to produce something new, mutant, and distinctly Brazilian. This theme infected much of the subsequent vanguard art. It is echoed in the work of attentive non-Brazilians new to that expansive country; a noteworthy example being the Italian-born architect and curator Lina Bo Bardi.

Amid the turmoil of the 1960s, Dom Hélder Câmara, Roman Catholic Archbishop of Olinda and Recife, addressed the need for greater equity in economic and political progress. He advocated for the people of the Northeast, his native region, seeking a sense of optimism for members of his flock estranged by politics and, simultaneously, Western materialism.

What might Andrade, Bo Bardi, or Câmara have made of the ongoing interventions implemented by the Swiss architects Herzog & de Meuron on behalf of the Ameropa Foundation in Mãe Luíza – an informal community in the northeastern city of Natal? Rather than some acultural imposition from afar, or some bureaucratic diktat, the multipart project emerged from its immediate context. It reutilized the fabric and structure of existing buildings; and amplified the grain of pathways and urban massing.

In aerial photographs, we see the physical placement of Mãe Luíza. The neighborhood established itself not far from the city center, along a hillside overlooking the Atlantic Ocean. That is an everyday reality in Brazil, a provisional urbanism independent of official planning or services yet benefitting from extraordinary views. The course adopted by the architects was to augment that reality and open up and intensify links within the community and between the community and its surroundings.

A heightened sense of place was achieved through the superior definition of built space and an embrace of nature. In Mãe Luíza, the architects envisioned a menu of interventions: better streets, a kind of public forum or agora, a low-slung building for communal and athletic activities, and a link out to a viewing platform from which the spectacular landmass and coastline are legible. That is where building optimism strengthened the community from within while also opening it up to the continental world.

How might architects from one culture operate – build – in another? For the exhibition *Building Optimism* at Pittsburgh's Heinz Architectural Center at the Carnegie Museum, 18 projects from across South America were presented, ranging from the strategic insertion of new institutions into the urban fabric of Medellín, Colombia, to a more dispersed proposal for commu-nity pavilions along the earthquake-prone coast of Chile. Such designs raised collective consciousness to civic benefit.

Like elsewhere in the world, many South American cities now host "signature buildings" by architects parachuted-in temporarily from abroad. Closely allied to product branding and commodification, such "starchitecture" can reduce architecture to the status of trinkets.

For the exhibition, only two projects by non-South American practices were included: Lima's robust UTEC university, a work of giant infrastructure by Dublin's Grafton Architects, and the incremental amelioration of Mãe Luíza by Herzog & de Meuron.

232   So, what do we mean by Building Optimism? What do we hope for by
      aligning ourselves with this phrase?

      Physical construction, of course; attention to building as both noun
      and verb, entailing close attention to the components of construction
      and the way components are assembled and reinforce one another.
      Optimism, therefore, not derived from any faux application of imagery
      or fashion; rather, the character of building and place resulting, at
      least in part, from a sequence of logical decisions – a sense of optimism
      resulting from a kind of poetic pragmatism.

      The word "building," used as a noun, refers to an object in the physical
      space of the city or countryside. But "building" is also a gerund, a
      grammar signifier of the act of building. Building, in this sense, is about
      creation with a strong suggestion of communal activity. That interpre-
      tation of building lessens the emphasis on some complete and finalized
      object and allows for imperfection and adaptability across time. There
      is optimism in both the goal and the process.

      Urban planning necessarily seeks to balance morphological legibility
      with the capacity for change or permutation. Architects can aim
      for buildings that are simultaneously precise and relaxed, conscious
      of form yet sufficiently informal to allow for modification and growth
      over time. Thus, in building optimism, there are aspects of the rational
      and the organic. Attention to the assembly of building components
      is allied with an appreciation of nature – the sunlight, shade, vegetation
      and ocean breezes so abundant along the Brazilian littoral.

      In such inductions of optimism, social space and cooperative buildings
      provide special opportunities. Facilities like the Arena do Morro, in the
      heart of Mãe Luíza, invite citizens to share experiences and encounter
      one another in ways denied by hermetic, single-use buildings.

233 Community spirit is an animating factor in such undertakings. After all, once the professional teams have completed their tasks, the building and its environs are in the care of the neighborhood and society. That sense of care continues long after completion of the physical project. The ultimate project is not merely the structure but, rather, the ways in which society grows to use the structure in multiple and inventive ways, making it Brazilian, in Andrade's words.

The form must always be adjusted by local reality, local technology and local modes of gathering. Success in Natal will be measured by how the people of Mãe Luíza make these interventions their own.

Perhaps, this mirrors Câmara's exhortation decades ago to "intervene in reality in order to change it."

Nicholas Fox Weber

Idealism

A "feet on the ground" idealism, based on a sense of solidarity and practical initiatives, is not something found on every corner. Rolling up one's sleeves and undertaking actions capable of changing people's lives for the better is what makes the difference.

"He's / She's such an idealist," we hear.

I don't know about you, but to me the statement sounds slightly pejorative. The implication is that the person being spoken about is not entirely practical. "Head in the clouds" is implicit. It is someone who is full of good wishes and airy-fairy theories absent a solid foundation and the practical know-how to put positive intentions into action.

Why must idealism get such a bum rap?

The example of Mãe Luíza makes idealism an altogether different thing. Since you are reading this book already, you may know the story by now, perhaps far better than I do, but I think it is worth retelling.

We will get there. First, however, there is a reason that idealism hits a very personal note. I was brought up by idealists – in the truest sense of the word. My father, born in 1915, and mother, born in 1919, developed a romance – Mom was 18 when they met, 19 when they married – based on idealism. The ideal was clear to both of them: there should be equality among human beings. Poor people should have more on which to live; no one should be oppressed because of racial or ethnic background; human beings should be kind to one another; fascism was something to overcome; no individual should dictate the way others lived. Their idealism was not necessarily in my DNA – in fact, I don't believe in such things, because all of us, whoever we are, have ancestors whose values we don't share – but it was in all that was said and done when I was a child. What was more important than genetics was what I heard and saw, because idealism has to be acted upon to make a difference.

It is not just that I saw my parents as romantic – although they were: my mother with her Lauren Bacall brand of womanliness, more strong than girly; my father with his swarthy looks and way of lighting a woman's cigarette by flicking his Dunhill lighter so speedily and quietly you only noticed it afterwards – but rather as linked by the desire for the betterment of humanity and the eradication of evil that defines idealism. Their engagement party was a fundraiser for the Abraham Lincoln Brigade, a small army of independent Americans who went to Spain to fight Franco and totalitarianism just as the opposite of idealism was taking hold in that beautiful country (after that, like Picasso, they would never travel to Spain while Franco was still alive). My mother wore wool stockings at their wedding so as not to have the slightest amount of money go towards buying Japanese silk at a time when Japan was trying to expand and therefore getting ready to wage war. They joined the American Communist Party – and, yes, this caused them to be fearful in the 1950s when Joseph McCarthy made it his mission to destroy all those who had considered anyone who believed that Communism might alleviate the pains of the poor and add equality to human existence. My parents had left the party by the time Stalin became head of the Soviet Union – they saw, as many idealists do, that power corrupts, and absolute power corrupts absolutely – but the ideals remained in their hearts.

So, of course the first time I learned about the project in Mãe Luíza, I felt an ease and connection; idealists seem like blood relatives to me. Like my parents – my father ran the printing company that my mother's father had started – all the support groups from Switzerland, Germany and Brazil (for details see pp. 268–271) depended on the successes of solidarity to make idealism action more than hollow words.

The initiative reached the most underserved with panache. People in need were given a leg up; this was how idealism was a game changer for many.

I suppose that one of the reasons this gets to me is that in my childhood, I saw too many idealists – my parents among them – essentially throw up their hands in despair. Communism begot totalitarianism:

236 it was czarist dictatorship in a different form. Then, horrifically, in the 1960s, John Fitzgerald Kennedy and Martin Luther King, two individuals full of heart and hope – and ideals – for millions of people, were brutally killed. To remain an idealist in the face of such setbacks to human progress requires committed individuals, unlike some academics who study idealism rather than act according to it. Theirs is the vocabulary of gobbledygook, with lengthy texts that define it as a combination of "metaphysical philosophies" and then use as a crutch academic lingo that insistently throws in words like "epistemologically," "ontological," "dualistic" and "phenomenologically." How about rolling up your sleeves and having idealism realized in a form that ameliorates hardship and lends joy to life every single day, as the Centro Sócio has done in Mãe Luíza?

One of the oldest conundrums in human thinking is why people are generous. Idealism, to me, is generosity realized: good works in action not just thoughts.

In *Of Human Bondage*, the brilliant English novelist and story writer Somerset Maugham sets up a conversation between the hero, Philip, and the worldly, over-confident artist named Cronshaw. In chapter XLV, Cronshaw says:

> "'Men seek but one thing in life – their pleasure.'
> 'No, no, no!' cried Philip.
> Cronshaw chuckled.
> 'You rear like a frightened colt, because I used a word to which your Christianity ascribes a deprecatory meaning. You have a hierarchy of values; pleasure is at the bottom of the ladder, and you speak with a little thrill of self-satisfaction, of duty, charity and truthfulness…. You would not be so frightened if I had spoken of happiness instead of pleasure: it sounds less shocking […] But […] It is pleasure that lurks in every one of your virtues. Man

performs actions because they are good for him, and when they are good for other people as well they are thought virtuous: if he finds pleasure in giving alms he is charitable; if he finds pleasure in helping others he is benevolent; if he finds pleasure in working for society he is public-spirited; but it is for your private pleasure that you give twopence to a beggar as much as it is for my private pleasure that I drink another whisky and soda. I, less of a humbug than you, neither applaud myself for my pleasure nor demand your admiration.'"

One of the easiest ways to retreat from idealism, which, after all, is best manifested in working for the larger world, is to be cynical about it. Maugham's dialogue is a delightful way of extolling the merits of empathy and consequent generosity by arguing against them. Because they are both idealistic and tenacious, the project participants in Mãe Luíza have braved the battle to help vast underserved populations. Idealism with traction is heavenly, not just as a theory or wish but as a force for the benefit of others.

Andrea Lorenzo Scartazzini

Music as Self-Empowerment and Identity

The Mãe Luíza Music School nurtures the dreams of young talents and has a positive impact on the whole community. The dedication of the Brass Band born here inspires the audience at neighborhood events and showcases music as an effective tool for professional training, the strengthening of self-esteem, and the formation of cultural identity.

238   Music, in all its exceptionally diverse styles and forms, is so omnipresent and taken for granted that we seldom give it much thought. Our constant companion, all too often it serves only to drown out the silence or the underlying buzz of everyday life. Music rolls over us and wraps itself around us wherever people gather – in shops, restaurants, bars and clubs, elevators, public transportation, city streets and squares, even at the beach, not to mention in advertisements and the media. It escapes from headphones, loudspeakers, radios and TV screens, and once in a while it comes to us live.

Music is with us from the day we are born, intimate and innocent at first, as lullabies and children's songs. Later, as the years go by, many of us develop a deeply personal relationship with music. We sing, hum, whistle, play and listen, and these melodies and sounds come to nest in our heads, insistent echoes adding a spring to our step, driving us on, lifting us up and consoling us. Are not some of the most profound, deeply felt, happiest and most moving moments tangled up with the sound of music? Music creates friendships, forms the basis of identity, strengthens our common bonds. Festive occasions without music, soccer triumphs without the fans' songs, culture without concerts, parties and dancing without rhythm and sound – "Life without music would be an error" (Friedrich Nietzsche).

Music is a profound secret. It is a language, but not a conventional one, since it reaches layers that words alone do not, and often does so with shattering intensity. Of all art forms, it is perhaps music that speaks to us most directly – regardless of age and education. And yet it is as individual in its effect as are people themselves. The same piece of music that moves one person to ecstasy leaves others cold.

Music brings us together across time and space: the melody to *Happy Birthday*, the song sung most often around the world, comes from the kindergarten teacher Mildred Hill of Louisville, Kentucky, who wrote it in 1893 for her collection of songs, *Song Stories for the Kindergarten*. Few can identify the author of the melody, but the song is sung in every corner of the world. It has become universal, as have many others that are bound up with rituals and traditions.

Music has the power to change and improve people's lives. That is probably why so many of us dream of a career as a star and idol of the masses and may well explain why for years we have seen talent and casting shows on every channel in every country.

Anyone who deals with music in a professional capacity knows how demanding and complex a subject it is. Music has a grammar (the theory of harmony) and an alphabet (musical notation). It also has a great many rules (which one should sometimes break). Learning to play and practice an instrument or undertake vocal training require, along with a gift for music, hard work and discipline. But investing such strength and energy pays off. Making music is fulfilling, and devoting oneself to music lends beauty, substance and meaning to life.

The virtues that this activity demands extend to other areas of life as well. To dedicate oneself to something with patience, to practice a sequence again and again, to improve steadily, to develop joy and ambition in the pursuit of challenging tasks (aspects that are equally fundamental in sports): all these qualities strengthen one's character and give shape to daily life well beyond the realm of the purely musical. It is then possible for one to pursue other goals as well in a more concentrated way, to make better use of one's time and to accept new challenges with greater determination.

Since 2018, Mãe Luíza has had a music school and since 2016 a Brass Band comprised of 35 young people. The school gives 75 children and young people the opportunity to learn how to play a wind instrument. There is enormous enthusiasm for this new institution, and acceptance

240 requires that one first pass an exam. As there are not enough instruments available for everyone, students have to share instruments in order to practice. The musicians play regularly at community events and a Mãe Luíza without its Brass Band has already become unthinkable. A number of especially gifted students have already been accepted by the Music School at the Federal University of Rio Grande do Norte.

As a social project, the Mãe Luíza Music School has also had a positive impact on the families of the young musicians: their passion and devotion to music prove irresistible to everyone around them. They also carry a message: that it is worthwhile to invest energy in oneself and one's own education, and that to begin a journey to a better life need not be an illusion. Viewed in this light, engaging with music is not simply a wonderful way to pass the time; it is an essential instrument of self-empowerment and identity.

Translated by Philip Hadock

Nicole Miescher

Fragility of the Project

Continuity of the work to transform Mãe Luíza depends as much on the will and readiness of the people involved as it does on the continued funding of activities and on the attitude of public authorities. This piece offers a reflection on risks and threats to the initiatives.

242

For more than 30 years, a group of women and men from the Centro Sócio in Mãe Luíza has been highly committed to fighting for the betterment of life of this poor community. They work on the basis of a modest salary or for free without any financial interest. They are driven by idealism and deeply believe that things, in reality, can be changed to the better. A number of friends from Brazil as well as Switzerland and Germany support them in their work and accompany them on their path.

Without the idealism of all the stakeholders, nothing would ever have happened.

But could this solid network one day fall apart? Will there be new people to carry on the work? Will the new people have the same passion, commitment and persistence?

Will the necessary funding continue to be provided?

Will politicians change construction laws for Mãe Luíza, allowing gentrification of this community, beautifully situated in the midst of Natal and the dunes overlooking the ocean? Will financial interests win over social considerations, forcing the people of Mãe Luíza to move to the periphery as in so many cases, to make room for upscale housing?

It appears that public authorities will remain absent and not comply with their responsibilities unless pressured to do so, or if there is a specific advantage in their doing something.

Luck is also part of life. We believe that with luck, perseverance and the continued will to fight, Mãe Luíza will find its way forward, as it has for the last three decades.

Mô Bleeker

Circle or Spiral: Reflections of an Anadromous Salmon

To what extent could the experience in Mãe Luíza be a source of inspiration for other poor communities in the Northeast of Brazil and elsewhere striving to achieve a modicum of dignity and autonomy for themselves? This was the question posed by the publishers of this book when we met for the first time. What could I say in response? I had never been to Mãe Luíza, had never walked upon its soil, smelled its odors, seen its sights, nor even heard the music of daily life in that community.

Since then, however, I have listened attentively to the many stories told about Mãe Luíza and, as I listened, an image came to mind that might describe its potential as a wellspring for transformation. At first, a vague, but round form took shape: the figure of a circle. The community as a sphere of awakening and solidarity. A circle of life. An inherently virtuous circle. On further reflection, however, the circle seemed too limited as a metaphor. By itself, the community could not sustain its own transformation, let alone be an inspiration for others. People suffer and people struggle. As a community, they may make some progress and attain some improvements, but fundamentally nothing really changes. Or does it?

I listened again and tried to retrace the steps that the community of Mãe Luíza had taken. Its strength lay in its ability to organize itself and engage collectively with others outside the community. In ever widening circles, Mãe Luíza reached out to other social actors, who themselves became transformed, creating the conditions for change in society at large. Gradually, the image of the circle recast itself into the figure of a spiral, a form of life that extends beyond itself. The question then became clear to me: How does a virtuous circle expand into a life-giving spiral?

So, here I am, at the end of this book – swimming like an anadromous salmon upstream and against the current – looking for an answer to this fundamental human question.

248   Let's recall: Forcibly displaced, the future inhabitants of Mãe Luíza, survivors of hunger and exclusion, decide one day to leave in search of a place where there would not just be water, but perhaps something more than that – God willing. What were they thinking of? That God exists? Still? Or that his silence was like the drought that had finally dried up their wells? And what do you call a situation in which one has to decide – suddenly and without delay – either to remain in place near one's ancestors and die of starvation or depart for the unknown, an act that may extend one's life, but may well result in a premature death due to unforeseen causes?

After much hardship, the displaced community arrives in the Northeast. They settle down behind a last big sand dune, the final barrier before the ocean. The place is called Alto da Aparecida. On a map, it looks like a small birth mark at the top of the right shoulder of Brazil. Settling first as squatters, their status remains ambivalent, until the mayor at that time, Djalma Maranhão, grants them the legal right to reside there. On January 23, 1958, Alto da Aparecida is formally recognized as the settlement of "Mãe Luíza," named after the first woman inhabitant and first mid-wife of the community. The settlement grows slowly, while remaining at a subsistence level. During this time, the military seizes power in Brazil.[1] In the Northeast, the dictatorship adds to the violence that already exists in multiple forms. There is structural violence, expressed through systematic exclusion, the negation of fundamental human rights, and the absence of the rule of law. Cultural violence is embedded in the ideology of national security, in racism, and in widespread discrimination. And finally, there is direct interpersonal violence: crimes of desperation rub shoulders with crimes generated by the dictatorship – torture, forced disappearances, as well as corruption and the lure of illegal gain through drug smuggling and human trafficking.[2] In Brazil, and especially in the Northeast, the opulence of the few presents a sharp contrast to the extreme poverty of the many. All in all, a hideous carnival of inhumanity.

The inhabitants of Mãe Luíza thus form part of a community that remains immensely vulnerable, still a community of survivors, without a name, without protection, at the mercy of the more powerful. Children are born, old people pass away – may they rest in peace. The young people also leave, attracted to other lights like moths around a flame: quick and easy money, drugs, crime, gangs, street fighting and their share of fear and death. The dangers change shape over the course of the years. Soon enough, this corner of paradise attracts its own breed of vultures: land speculators who want to enjoy an exclusive view of the ocean without being disturbed by these poor squatters, those non-consumers whom it would be better to expel in any case – literally – beyond the sandy beaches of a voracious modern society. Landslides also hit Mãe Luíza with full force, destroying livelihoods and sometimes lives as well. Mãe Luíza reconstructs and Mãe Luíza rebuilds – too often a labor of Sisyphus.

Inspired by the sermons of Dom Hélder Câmara, Archbishop of Olinda and Recife, 200 km to the south, and his call for history *to be dreamed, enacted, and written as a common endeavor,* Mother and Father Courage emerge in this community and remind each other of the importance of sharing, of respecting oneself and others, of their common dignity. Almost everywhere in Brazil, particularly in the North-east, and more broadly in Latin America, a similar wind is blowing. In the face of a State that is absent, corrupt, or authoritarian, communities see a need to fight for the recognition of their rights, to organize them-selves in such a way that goes beyond mere survival, in order to live life in dignity. In the wake of popular campaigns of literacy and the promotion of public health, hundreds of young people, adult women and men, lay persons and members of religious orders leave their places of residence, often in urban areas, and discover with amazement the daily reality of millions of their fellow citizens, who suffer from hunger and a thousand other opportunistic diseases of poverty and illiteracy. People without rights and without a voice. The call *to stand up and resist*

250 is being heard throughout Latin America and on other continents as well. But what does it mean *to stand up and resist*? To pass from a state of mere survival to that of living in dignity is a complicated process. Difficult and, at first glance, literally unimaginable.

It is here, in this essentially nameless territory of the in-between, a place of transition between current and imagined identities, that a collective and horizontal impulse takes hold and launches an upheaval that continues to this day. The women, men, young people, and children of Mãe Luíza – forced migrants and squatters – are again on the road, but this time it is, above all, an inner migration, the metamorphosis of marginalized human beings without a proper destiny into social subjects and the subjects of rights. The transformation of an improbable group of bruised individuals into a community of identities, of lives, of interests, of struggle, marks a point of departure and a finish line, a meeting place, a place of alchemy. Like numerous communities in the Northeast, elsewhere in Brazil and in Latin America, Mãe Luíza becomes a fostering and fertile community, a place of belonging, a place of identity affirmation. Life there remains harsh and rudimentary, public services are insufficient and violence always rife. Yet, there is an immense energy present, an emancipatory spirit that produces change – other ways of imagining oneself and one's reality.

The metamorphosis that has begun is contagious in a positive sense. Those who come from the outside are intrigued and inspired, and – why not say it – literally *fascinated and enchanted*. Above all, however, they are challenged: Philanthropy can help, but it cannot transform. It can provide, as it were, a sterile dressing for a wound, but it cannot heal the wound itself. In essence, it is an insufficient remedy. And beware: Philanthropy cannot and must not attempt to replace a negligent and absent State, which chooses to ignore its duty to serve the common good.

When Padre Sabino comes to live in Mãe Luíza, numerous friends and volunteers join him to share a moment of life. They understand that *to be with*, *to march with* those who stand up and resist, one must go a step further. Perhaps they also share the conviction that "[…] no one teaches another, nor is anyone self-taught. Men teach each other, mediated by the world."[3] Visitors from other parts of Brazil and from the world at large arrive, impressed by the inhabitants of Mãe Luíza and touched by this energy. Foreign assistance is now also present and provides financial support for the collective initiatives arising from the mobilization of community members, including an elementary school, a preschool, a center for the elderly, a community center, and a music school. In collaboration with the community, Herzog and de Meuron, the flagship of Swiss architecture, designs the Arena do Morro gymnasium, a project that will appear on the covers of the most prestigious architectural journals in the world. At the same time, the Ameropa Foundation, established by the Basel-based multinational grain and fertilizer company of the same name, finances the construction of social infrastructure in Mãe Luíza.

When the visitors return home, they speak about the community: about Padre Sabino, the beauty of the people and of the countryside, and the poverty that does not go away. They also say that certain things are getting better. And what else do they talk about? About simple things mostly. That in Mãe Luíza people look at the why and how of things differently – the matters of daily life, of sadness, of *"saudade,"* or of hope. That people say that the sense of fatalism, which has always accompanied them, is fading and that something still indistinct, which does not yet have a name, is replacing it, little by little. A presentment gradually spreads that *something else, another life* is possible. That to be poor, whether black or indigenous, in the Northeast, in Brazil, in the world, does not have to be a curse. Padre Sabino, the Brazilian, Swiss, and German friends, the Ameropa Foundation – they also feel this, vaguely at first, each in her or his own way, each in her or his own words. That which in common to them all, however, is what they experience in Mãe Luíza. It is what gives them meaning, what adds a new sense of direction to their lives, though hardly perceived at this time. And so, it is: Mãe Luíza creates an abundance of meaning.

In the settlement, people share what they know. They learn from each other. They also engage in dialog to better understand the context into which they are born, in which they live. As Maurice Godelier, the French social anthropologist, writes, people do not only live in society; they produce society in order to live. They construct history. Of the two forces which make up the power of domination and exploitation, the strongest is not the violence exercised by the institutions or classes which dominate a society, but the consent of those who submit to their domination.[4] If there had been consent in this case, it quickly dissipates when the community of Mãe Luíza begins to understand that extreme poverty is neither a disease nor a hereditary disability. Instead, it is the result of a number of political, social, and economic factors. What is not normal is the fact that the State has been so negligent, that there is no infrastructure in the settlement – neither a plan for development nor any work in that direction worthy of the name. No, it is not normal. All the more so, as those politicians, who insist that the members of the community vote for them (addressing them at this moment only as "citizens"), have already promised so many things – one promising to create a public health center, another a school or paved roads. But the promises dissipate with the morning sea breezes and nothing follows. Nothing remains but mistrust and a profound sense of injustice.

So, learning to write a simple word – WATER, for example – initiates a debate about any number of questions that they discuss together: Where does water come from? Why is some water fresh and other water salty? What about rainwater? And water from tears? Why do we say that women "break water" before giving birth? Why say that *one drinks the water of the baby* when celebrating its birth? Who owns the water?

Is it harmful to health? How do we purify it? Why are there no toilets? Then, decline a noun such as "education," "health," "woman," "equality," "participation," "state responsibility," and all sorts of questions arise that demand action. When reality becomes *intelligible*, we become stronger and we are more aware of what we have to do and of how to proceed. Conjugate the verb "to be" "I am" and "we are." Then the pronouns "my" and "our," i.e. "my" life – "our" destiny, "my" children – "our" education, "my" grandparents – "our" culture, but "our" rights – "their" duties.

And what about the Constitution of the Federative Republic of Brazil! What a magnificent preamble, veritable music for the soul. It contains such delicate phrases that the whole passage seems embroidered by hand: "[…] a democratic state for the purpose of ensuring the exercise of social and individual rights, liberty, security, well-being, development, equality and justice as supreme values of a fraternal, pluralist and unprejudiced society, founded on social harmony and committed, in the internal and international orders, to the peaceful settlement of disputes."[5] What a plan! If one were to attempt to "comprehend" (Latin: "com-prehendere" or "com-prendere" – to "bind together," i.e. to "grasp as a whole") the meaning of each word of this preamble? And if one were to make it a reality? But where is this State that should be its guarantor and promoter? What is it doing? Is there any way of explaining to those officials that they are not respecting the Constitution? Who could do that? And what would this mean for Mãe Luíza?

Mãe Luíza is becoming more inclusive and welcoming. The feeling of belonging generates a sense of joy and pride, of cultural identity expressed in music, song, theater, and life stories. Those who go around armed with guns know it – the law of force and violence is losing ground. Something is happening in Mãe Luíza. It is not like it was before. And would the practice of participatory budgeting be introduced following the example of Porto Alegre,[6] the community would learn to plan for the common good, to combine public welfare with free time activity, collective investments with the distribution of goods, and the fight against corruption with the rule of law. In short, an inventory of possibilities as intoxicating as the thousands of constellations that they can see when they lie on the ocean beach and open their eyes on a moonless night. So, swimming back up the river, the anadromous salmon asks itself what we have learned so far? What is special, even inspiring, about the case of Mãe Luíza and about this odd combination of commitment and goodwill?

Let us dismiss from the outset the label "idealism," often enough synonymous with admiration from a safe distance, rendering the object of esteem both *"salonfähig"* (socially acceptable) and convenient. And give a final wave of the hand to all the other "-isms" as well. These labels lack subtilty and evoke biases, which some people use haphazardly and without distinction to compare those who offer some spare time with those who devote their whole lives to the community or those who donate some surplus supplies with those who organize communal meals for the inhabitants of Mãe Luíza. The ideological arguments of political parties are not more persuasive, whether they stem from "revolutionary" parties, often themselves authoritarian, hierarchical, and patriarchal, or from more "progressive" ones. Dom Hélder Câmara described this well: "When I fed the poor, they called me a saint. When I asked, 'Why are they poor?' they called me a communist."[7] The DNA of the communitarian dynamics of emancipation, which is developing in Mãe Luíza and, in a similar manner, in other communities in Brazil's Northeast, in Latin America, and in other places in the world, where exclusion and poverty go hand in hand, cannot be captured by reductionist labels. The fact is that, at some point and for a variety of reasons, communities *no longer consent*. They organize themselves to attain their rights and demand that the State assume its responsibilities.

What do we know then about those who live in Mãe Luíza? That progressively they open their eyes, that they begin to *see* themselves differently and thus produce *a different reality*. Simply put: *they realize who they are and who they can become*. Inspiration begins with the discovery of one's own identity in a particular social, cultural, and structural context. It results in the appropriation of one's own history and therefore of one's own future as well. What "I" means in this society; what "we" means. "My" commitment, "our" common struggle.

And when Padre Sabino meets this community, he immediately perceives its potential – its *inherent* potential. He also knows that they must work together in order for the progress to be sustainable; cooperate on a horizontal level to such an extent that, when he dies, the commitment to a collective spirit can naturally live on because it is shared by everyone. And when the president of the Ameropa Foundation visits Mãe Luíza, she immediately understands the uniqueness of what is taking place – something so profoundly and deeply human that she decides that the Foundation should support this effort. For a philanthropic institution, it is a welcome opportunity, a judicious choice, and a wise investment. Indeed, when communities are organized, the impact of any financial support is multiplied.

In its catalogue, Herzog and Meuron writes that the large roof which covers the Arena do Morro gymnasium serves as a metaphor of the community – a space that is open to receive all.[8] Indeed, no one would deny that beauty contributes to the recovery of dignity and to the renewal of public space in cities. Others have understood this as well. At the same time, under different circumstances, with more or less community involvement and support of the State, the reconquest of public spaces is taking place in other locations marked by poverty, violence, and discrimination. In Colombia, for example, well-known architect Rogelio Salmona is supporting the transformation of *"comunas de la violencia"* in Medellín into safe spaces accessible to everyone, and "non-spaces" in Bogotá into places for peaceful gatherings and cultural exchange. Not surprisingly, therefore, we hear that gang

256 members deposit their weapons at the entrance to Arena Do Morro to engage in a sporting event before rejoining the struggle in the streets. Like the members of the terrible Mara Salvatrucha, a small-town gang in El Salvador, winning the medal for the most beautiful flower arrangement during Easter festivities – a magnificent carpet of flowers, celebrating the beauty of Maria or the beauty of their mother, who knows? Just for the period of a cease-fire. And it is true: beauty humanizes and beauty spurns violence, but only briefly, if not accompanied by vigorous social policies.

So, we see a wonderful, virtuous circle taking shape; at the same time, however, we know its cruel limitations. As in every closed circle, everything stays where it is. The laws of exclusion, as unchangeable as the laws of gravity, reproduce themselves again and again. Whether the members of the community are playing basketball or giving a concert under the vast roof of the Arena do Moro, the State is still failing to fulfill its responsibilities. Mãe Luíza remains vulnerable, exposed to the capricious winds of political turnabout, to greed and corruption, to the laws of profit and inflation, to a murderous escalation in gang violence, or even to lassitude on the part of the community. For a transformation to take place effectively and to be sustainable, a number of important actors, indeed all concerned parties, need to be involved. As long as major players, such as the State and the private sector, continue to deny responsibility, it is difficult to imagine how this process of transformation could become sustainable. In fact, the local, regional, and national governments have failed again and again – by action and by omission – to meet their obligations and duties. Yet, it is well-known that cooperation between accountable public institutions and participatory community organizations accelerates the process of transformation and often produces lasting results. Over time, well-placed and judicious investments in public development policy can transform an entire society by prioritizing poverty reduction, improvement of public health services, vocational training, and other preferential measures. This is also the reason why the Sustainable Development Goals,[9] as formulated by the United Nations and jointly promoted by the international community, specifically aim to support a dynamic of interdependence between governments and citizens as *duty-bearers* and *right-holders*, respectively, that – well understood – could produce durable change in societal structures and relations.

At this stage of our reflection, another narrative is still missing. That of a third actor, which plays a unique and important role: the private sector. As the United Nations reminds us in its reflection about the role of the private sector in promoting the Sustainable Development Goals, it is "in its own self-interest" to fully support the advancement of the rule of law, so as to strengthen a functional system of justice and the respect for human rights, both in the countries in which it operates, and globally.[10] To this end, the UN calls upon the business community to sign and implement the Ten Principles of the UN Global Compact.[11] Numerous multinational corporations and private businesses are currently working in Brazil. They play a significant role in the country's development. Their presence or absence, their voice or their silence have an important impact on the government and on national policy. In other words, the private sector, especially in the case of international corporations, is well-positioned to pressure the government in favor of policies promoting social and economic justice by conditioning its investments or engagement. Moreover, it would be *in its own self-interest* to do so, all the more so because the situation today in Brazil is so bleak. It is estimated by the World Bank that more than 12 million people currently live in a state of extreme poverty.[12] Hunger is again prevalent throughout the country. Without adequate social programs and in the face of a looming health crisis, that number could increase by some 70% in the next four years. At the same time, the country is also facing an ecological crisis. The number of forest fires in the Amazon basin of Brazil in 2020 rose by almost 20% in comparison to the previous year. The indigenous populations are the primary victims.

258 Not to mention the loss of flora and fauna. Numerous regions, like Mãe Luíza as a coastal community, are already suffering the consequences of the climate crisis, while the rest of the planet is witnessing one of its vital organs go up in smoke.

Something radically inconsistent is happening here, the anadromous salmon tells itself. The scales are not balanced, the equation does not add up. It does not seem fair to place the entire burden of its transformation solely on the shoulders of the community of Mãe Luíza, even with the kind support of its numerous friends. Justice demands more: it requires an equally strong commitment on the part of all to ensure that the State and the private sector assume their respective responsibilities *vis à vis* the social contract established by the Brazilian Constitution and the UN Global Compact.[13] To continue this game of solitaire, in which each player continues to play the same role, *alone and isolated*, ad infinitum, is to act in a closed circle. It does not make sense and could, in fact, result in a new cycle of victimization in Mãe Luíza. On the contrary, it would be important to mobilize the sense of responsibility among those in government and in the private sector, and promote a true dialog between them and the community of Mãe Luíza. And, by the way, Mãe Luíza is ready for such an exchange. It has drafted – in a participatory manner – its own plan for development, a useful tool to engage in dialogue with candidates running for election, with public authorities, with the private sector.[14]

And if this community has been able to reinvent itself under extremely difficult conditions, if these women and men have stood up, is it too far-fetched to imagine that, in the wake of this example, the private sector and the government would also stand up and finally exercise their responsibility as full members of the global community, as subjects of rights and of duties? In short, that they should also be inspired by Mãe Luíza?

But, let us return to Switzerland where the Ameropa Foundation and its parent company, Ameropa, are based. In the same vein as above, we propose that they take another preamble, namely that of the Swiss Constitution, as an additional source of inspiration for their initiatives in Brazil and elsewhere in the world, since governance, economy, and climate do not figure just at a national level, but also globally. The text of this preamble is equally magnificent, just as delicately hand-embroidered and, on top of everything else, carries the "made in Switzerland" label, which is to say that it would be *in our own self-interest* to practice today on a global scale: "(The Swiss people) [...] determined to live together with mutual consideration and respect for their diversity, conscious of their common achievements and their responsibility towards future generations, and in the knowledge that only those who use their freedom remain free, and that the strength of a people is measured by the well-being of its weakest members...."[15]

At a time when Brazil is burning, Mãe Luíza is still very vulnerable indeed. Yet, the history of Mãe Luíza is truly a remarkable source of inspiration, and if the women and men of Mãe Luíza succeed in completing their incredible metamorphosis into dignified human beings, what would each one of us be capable of achieving, here and now – if we were to let ourselves be truly inspired – and transformed? If we were to set ourselves decidedly and without respite to the task of transforming our society and its structures to arrive at the eagerly awaited goal of shared responsibility for the benefit of the common good?

Nothing is unthinkable. As proof, if this community of survivors is able to produce human dignity in abundance, one could expect that the government and the private sector would also be capable of entering into a dynamic of real partnership and, by way of fulfilling their joint responsibility, that they would engage in a virtuous spiral for the public welfare. Such partnerships have the potential to increase the quality of community life, i.e. *sustainable* community life, in which social relations

260

are supportive and caring, and which foster an interdependence on a global scale, in which "the strength of a people is measured by the well-being of its weakest members."

And if we also open our eyes – *in our own collective interest* – and we also stand up, what would happen? Specifically, today in Brazil, in Switzerland, in the world? Today. Here. Me. Us.

The salmon, then, nestling at the source of the river, takes a last deep breath before descending on its path back to the sea. Weighing whether it still has the strength and then leaving behind a last trail of air bubbles that rise to the surface like so many concentric circles, transforming into spirals, losing themselves in the universal flow of life.

Translated by Jonathan Sisson

261

1 The military dictatorship lasted from April 1, 1964 to March 15, 1985. An account of the serious human rights violations that took place in Brazil between 1946 and 1988, especially during the period of the military dictatorship, was provided by the National Truth Commission (Comissão Nacional da Verdade), which published its report on December 10, 2014. For a summary of the report and its main recommendations (in English), see: Kai Ambos and Eneas Romero, "The Report of the Brazilian Truth Commission: Late Truth without Justice?" *EJIL: Talk!* (blog), January 19, 2015, accessed on February 18, 2021, https://www.ejiltalk.org/12892/. The full report (in Portuguese) can be accessed at: http://cnv.memoriasreveladas.gov.br/audi%C3%AAncias-p%C3%BAblicas.html

2 Johan Galtung's "triangle of violence" provides a useful framework to characterize the different facets of violence employed by the military dictatorship. See: Johan Galtung, "Violence, Peace and Peace Research," *Journal of Peace Research* 6, no. 3, (1969): 167–191 and Johan Galtung, "Cultural Violence," *Journal of Peace Research* 27, no. 3 (1990): 291–305.

3 Paulo Freire, *Pedagogy of the Oppressed* (New York: Seabury Press, 1974) 67.

4 Maurice Godelier, *L'Idée et le Matériel – Pensée,* Économie et Société, (Paris: Fayard, 1984) 9, 23–24.

5 "Federative Republic of Brazil 1988 Constitution with 1996 reforms," Political Database of the Americas, accessed on February 18, 2021, https://pdba.georgetown.edu/Constitutions/Brazil/english96.html#mozTocId324543

6 Participatory budgeting is practiced in many parts of Brazil and elsewhere in Latin America.

7 This saying is widely attributed to Hélder Câmara without a specific source given. For a selection of his writings, see Francis McDonagh (ed.), "Dom Hélder Câmara. Essential writings," (Maryknoll: Orbis, 2009).

8 https://www.herzogdemeuron.com/index/projects/complete-works/351-375/354-1-arena-do-morro.html

9 "Take Action for the Sustainable Development Goals – United Nations Sustainable Development," United Nations, accessed on February 18, 2021, https://www.un.org/sustainabledevelopment/sustainable-development-goals/.

10 "Business and SDG 16: Contributing to Peaceful, Just and Inclusive Societies," United Nations Sustainable Development Goals Fund, accessed on February 18, 2021, https://www.sdgfund.org/sites/default/files/Report_Business_And_SDG16.pdf

11 "The Ten Principles of the UN Global Compact," United Nations Global Compact, accessed on February 18, 2021, https://www.unglobalcompact.org/what-is-gc/mission/principles

12 Cited by Bruno Villas Bôas in: "Crise pode jogar mais 5,7 milhões na pobreza extrema no país," *Valor Econômico,* April 19, 2020, accessed on February 18, 2021, https://valor.globo.com/brasil/noticia/2020/04/19/crise-pode-jogar-mais-57-milhoes-na-pobreza-extrema-no-pais.ghtml

13 The UN urges companies engaged in the private sector to sign the Global Compact on a voluntary basis. The participating companies pledge to integrate the Ten Principles into their business strategy, culture and day-to-day operations. Moreover, these companies are required to report to their stakeholders on an annual basis about their progress in implementing the Principles and their efforts to support societal priorities. In its Code of Conduct, Ameropa, the parent company of the Ameropa Foundation, states that it "voluntarily abides by the UN Global Compact initiative." However, it does not state that it has actually signed the Global Compact nor does its name appear in the list of signatory companies on the Global Compact website. See: "The Ameropa Code of Conduct, Human Rights", Ameropa, accessed on February 18, 2021, https://www.ameropa.com/fileadmin/user_upload/About_Us/Ameropa_Code_of_Conduct_3.10.2018-1.pdf

14 See the description of the social network *Rede Inclusão e Direito à Cidade (Rede Inclusão)* and its activities on the website of Centro Sócio: http://centrosociopastoral.org.br/Rede_Inclusao/ (accessed on February 18, 2021).

15 Federal Constitution of the Swiss Confederation of 18 April 1999 (Status as of January 1, 2018), accessed on February 18, 2021, https://fedlex.data.admin.ch/filestore/fedlex.data.admin.ch/eli/cc/1999/404/20180101/en/pdf-a/fedlex-data-admin-ch-eli-cc-1999-404-20180101-en-pdf-a.pdf

Acknowledgements

264 **Brazil**

List of individuals who worked at the Centro Sócio over the years, from 1988 (hired or assigned)

Silva Fransueide Alves de Araújo
Marjane Maria Alves Ferraz
Allyson Amílcar Ângelo Freire Soares
Ion Garcia Mascarenhas de Andrade
Iracy Garcia Mascarenhas de Andrade
Caetano Joana de Araújo
Castro da Silva Rafael Edval de Araújo
Felipe Francisco de Araújo
Iara de Araújo
João Paulo Araújo
Lindalva Maria de Aráujo
Reis José Jerônimo de Araújo
Diana de Araújo Silva
Adriana Cláudia de Assis
Ana Lúcia de Assis
Anísio Roberto de Assis
Dayana do Nascimento Vieira
 de Assis
Francisco de Assis de Souza
Francisco de Assis Nascimento
 de Castro
Francisco de Assis Pereira de Morais
Jairo José Azevedo da Silva
José de Azevedo Joailson
Hilton de Azevedo Silva
Suerda Balbino Vieira
Juliana Balduíno dos Santos
Gidyonne Christine Bandeira Silva
Lucileide Barbosa da Silva
Alcione Barbosa de Lima
Ozete Barbosa de Moura Souza
Gentil Barbosa do Nascimento
Francisco Eduardo Barbosa
Geisa Barbosa Marinho
Luciana Barbosa Marinho
Domingo Barsa Soares
Luíza Belarmino de Oliveira
 (In Memoriam)
Aldenise Bernardino da Silva
Deise Bernardino da Silva
Iriane Maria Bernardo da Silva
Marinês Bertuleza Cunha da Silva
Francisca Darc Bezerra de Assis
Divanete Bezerra Santos de França
Iraneide de Franca Borges
Hermínio Pereira de Brito
Ana Heloiza Cassimiro Costa
Francisca das Chagas Silva

Gerinaldo Chianca da Fonseca
Lúcia Helena Coelho Nobrega
Maria da Conceição do Nascimento
Antonia da Conceição Lima Xavier
Maria da Conceição Silvania
Ana Paula Cordeiro da Silva
Sheny Alida Coriolano Monteiro
Maria do Socorro Correia Silva
 de Lima
Moelma Cortez de Medeiros
Vilaneide Cortez de Medeiros
Adriano Costa da Silva
Joseane Costa da Silva
José Jackson da Costa
José Roberto da Costa
Denise Cruz da Cunha
Gilson da Cruz
Marcelo Karlane da Cruz
Maria Francinalva Cunha
Maria Dantas da Silva (In Memoriam)
Carlos Magno Dantas de Medeiros
Jeann Karlo Dantas Lima
Daniel Denysin de Sena Ribeiro
Máximo Dias de Araújo
Valéria Dionizio Duarte
Joseane Domingos da Silva Gomes
Rosimary dos Santos Oliveira
Rosana Célia Dourado Grecco
Josinaldo Euflasino Salviano
Odair José Euflasino Salviano
José Carlos Euflausino
Francisco Canindé Faustino de Lira
Francisca Felicia Lima Rodrigues
Geisa Felicia Rodrigues de Lima
Inacia Patrícia Felix Miranda de Farias
Isabelle Katherinne Fernandes Costa
José Claudio Ferreira da Silva
Simone Fonseca Silveira
Francinalda Lima do Nascimento
Maria do Monte Freire do Nascimento
João Batista de Freitas
Vanessa Giffoni de M. N. Pinheiro
João Batista de Góis Filho
Ana Cláudia Gomes
Kátia Patrícia Gomes da Silva
Jaqueline Gomes Felipe da Cruz
João Batista Gomes Soares
Josilma Gomes Soares
José Guedes Filho
José Guedes
Joseniz Guimarães de Moura
Ivanildo Hermínio de Lima
Maria de Lourdes Inácio dos Santos
Luana Cibely Leandro dos Santos

Iranédia Lemos de Almeida
Carlos Alex de Lima
Maria das Graças Lima de Medeiros
Nágima Lima de Oliveira
Silva Francineide Lima do Nascimento
Maria da Conceição de Lima Ferreira
Jorge Lopes da Silva
Francisco Lucena de Araujo
Junior Luiz Marinho
Rosane Medeiros da Silva
José Mendes Feitosa
Edione Mendonça Macário
Edjane Mendonça Macário
Janny Kelly Monteiro Freire
Elizabeth Morais da Costa
Enaide Morais da Costa
Maria do Socorro Mota Coutinho
Adriana Maria do Nascimento
Antonio Cristiano do Nascimento
Francinalda do Nascimento Cardoso
Maria Tereza do Nascimento Caval-
 canti (In Memoriam)
Cláudia Maria do Nascimento
Redja Cristiane Nascimento
 de Oliveira
Juliane Iasmin do Nascimento
 Ferreira
Francineide do Nascimento
Maria das Dores do Nascimento
Maria Francisca do Nascimento
 (In Memoriam)
Marly do Nascimento
Sandra Maria do Nascimento
Isanilda Nogueira Bezerra
Maria do Socorro Nunes Chagas
Angélica Nunes Medeiros
Maria de Oliveira Barbosa Jailde
Célia Maria Oliveira da Silva
Maria dos Navegantes de Oliveira
Iole Bárbara de Oliveira Sbrana
Giovana Paiva Oliveira
Roseane Paula Veras da Costa
Maria Ednalva Paulo
Dione Paz Bezerra
Nélio Paz Bezerra
Geneci Pereira da Costa
Girlene Pereira da Costa
José Pereira de Brito Neto Gutemberg
José Pereira dos Reis Neto
Iara Pereira Matias Lopes
Bruna Carollina Pessoa de Macedo
Loyse Madeleine Raboud M.
 de Andrade
Jefferson Leandro Ramos de Oliveira

Acknowledgements

266

Marta Maria Castanho Almeida
 Pernambuco (In Memoriam)
Ana Célia Cavalcanti
Jessé Dantas Cavalcanti (In Memoriam)
João Helder Cavalcanti
Crinaura Maria (In Memoriam)
Marcus Vinícius de Faria Oliveira
Maria Virgínia Ferreira Lopes
Jean Luc Julien Gentil
Maria Fátima Jorge de Oliveira
Thales Thaynan Lemos Saldanha
 de Araújo
Ubiratan de Lemos
Verner Max Liger de Mello Monteiro
Francisca Iara Lopes Soares
Iedson Marques do Nascimento
Lúcio Medeiros
Marjorie da Fonseca e Silva Medeiros
Hermano Morais
Maria Gloria do Nascimento
Paulo Roberto Palhano Silva
Vinicius Pessoa Albino
Maria Bernadete Pinheiro
Álvaro José Pires Júnior
Elisabeth Raboud (In Memoriam)
Jean-Joseph Raboud
Eleika de Sá Bezerra
Lerson Fernando dos Santos Maia
Ivanildo Soares da Silva
Ernandes Teixeira

**State Secretariat of Education,
Culture and Sports / SECD**

Patricia Luz de Macedo
Ana Zélia Maria Moreira
Martha Vargas Soliz

**Municipal Secretariat of Environment
and Urbanism / SEMURB**

Ana Karla Galvão
Carlos Eduardo da Hora
Daniel Nicolau
Ruy Pereira (In Memoriam)
Rosa de Fátima de Souza

Fellow contributors

Iwan Baan
Christian Bannholzer

Vitoria Barbosa
Bianca de Bocage
Anna Ferrari
Leonadi Finotti
Manuel Herz
Heiko Klemme
Erik Schoen
Xenia Vytuleva-Herz

Switzerland

The Ameropa Foundation

Board 2001–2019
Nicole Miescher (co-founder and
 president)
Andreas Zivy (co-founder)

Board as of 2019
Céline Miescher (president)
Alix Zacharias
Nina Zivy

**Members and friends
of the Association of Friends
of Mãe Luíza**

Melinda Bellwald Terrettaz
Isabelle Bruchez
Laurent Bruchez
Alain Collioud
Brigitte Fontannaz
Anne Pascale Galletti
Jean Jacques Howald
Michèle Howald
Odile Maury
Muriel Paccolat
Monique Paini
Dominique Perraudin
Edwige Perraudin
François (Tounet) Perraudin
Isabelle Raboud
Suzanne Raboud
Yves Raboud
Georgette Reuse
Anne Terrettaz
Claude Terrettaz
Maryline Terrettaz
Victor Terrettaz (In memoriam)
Corinne Tornay
Pierre Tornay

People and entities that contributed
throughout the 25 years of partnership
of the Association of Friends of
Mãe Luíza, founded in April 1995

Club Archytas
Gérard Reymond
Sylvaine Rémy Association
 Constellation
Fernand Terrettaz
Jean Philippe Terrettaz

**Herzog & De Meuron
"A Vision for Mae Luíza," 2009 and
Arena do Morro, 2010–2014**

Partners
Jacques Herzog
Pierre de Meuron
Ascan Mergenthaler (partner-in-charge)
Markus Widmer

Project Team
Tomislav Dushanov (associate,
 project director)
Mariana Vilela (project manager)
Diogo Rabaça Figueiredo
Melissa Shin
Stephen Hodgson
Caesar Zumthor
Daniel Fernández Florez
Kai Strehlke (digital technologies)
Edyta Augustynowicz (digital
 technologies)

**Swiss interns who worked
at the Centro Sócio**

Marlene Barbosa
Vincent Bircher
Stephanie Dessimoz
Céline Dufner
Melanie Grutzner
Nicolas Gubler
Eric Hildenbeutel
Nathalie Howald Silva do Nascimento
Jocelyne Jean Jacquet Perrin
Martina Kiess
Aude Neuenschwander
Nathalie Nicollerat Gabioud
Lionel Perraudin
Aline Raboud de Oliveira Santos

Elizabeth Raichenbach
Clélie Riaz
Marielle Rupp
Salomé Steinman
Maud Terrettaz

Young people from the Bagnes Valley region who participated in urbanization of the Favela do Sopapo, which is now the Brisa do Mar Housing Project

Sarah Abbet
Raphaelle Bessard
Pierre Yves Bourgeois
David Chaton
Beatrice Fellay
Claudine Frossard
Damien Frossard
Delphine Frossard
Marc Frossard
Michel Frossard
Myriam Frossard
Viviane Gabioud
Boris Michellod
Fabien Terrettaz
Frédéric Terrettaz
Jean Philippe Terrettaz
Nicolas Terrettaz
Pascal Tornay

Trainees from Abroad

Heide Hollands (The Netherlands)
Sérgy Khudenko (Russia)
Frank Sweetman (Canada)

Germany

Friends of Padre Sabino

Pfarrer Konrad Albrecht
Barbara Braunmüller
Ignaz Dreyer
Josef and Rosa Drüszler
Barbara Höcherl
Johanna and Alfred Mayer
Maria Stoppel
Dorothee Teufel
Agathe and Friedel Zitar

Trainees from Germany

Isabelle Brunner
Katharina Diener
Barbara Fischer
Gabriela Konrad
Carsten Löb
Christiane Lubus
Nina Matschl

Partnership Mãe Luíza Penzberg E.V.

Monika Aigner
Ernst and Gabi Amschler
Benedikt Bernhard
Willi Berchtold
Manfred and Brigitte Fischer
Bertold Grolig
Irmi Obermeier and Johannes Deiss
Joachim and Ingrid Keller
Gerd and Margot Klose
Gisela and Klaus Matschl
Paula Nagel
Wilma Nitsch
Alessa Peuker
Pfarrer Josef Kirchensteiner
Gerhard Prantl
Ulrike Schulte-Kulkmann
Isabella Watzlawek
Alexandra Zirn

Eine-Welt Laden Penzberg (One-World-Shop Penzberg)

All "store women"
Barbara Braunmüller
Regina Herele
Angelika Siebert
Dorle Thanbichler

Choirs performing at GOSPELS & MORE for the benefit of Mãe Luíza

Regenbogen (Peiting)
Spirit of Generations (Penzberg)
Spiritual Profanists (Weilheim)

Partnership of St. Michael, Kochel AM SEE

Erwin and Veronika Fleissner
Sandra Heigl
Hubertus Klingebiel
Pia Pössenbacher
Barbara Samm

Frauengemeinschaft Mülhausen (Women's Community Mülhausen)

Inge Duffner and friends

Brasilienhilfe Eggenthal

Christiane Beer
Franz and Angelika Binn
Remigius and Rosina Kirchmaier
Hanni Steidele
Sabine Straber
Lisa Trem

When so many people are involved in a project over such a long period of time, it is possible, and indeed likely, that someone was forgotten or not recognized in the correct function. The editors ask for understanding.

List of Main Supporters

Switzerland

The Ameropa Foundation

In 2001 Ameropa, an international family-owned company, founded the Ameropa Foundation.

The Foundation supports humanitarian projects in developing countries. With a long-term approach, focus is given to entrepreneurial projects, education for children, adolescents, and adults as well as projects promoting culture and sport, thus giving local people the possibility to be able to realize a dream, and providing them with a concrete perspective to advance in life. Over the last 20 years, the Foundation has started and partially handled 53 projects. By the end of 2020, the number of beneficiaries had reached more than 100,000 people, there were ca. 5,000 jobs created, and more than 60,000 children, adolescents and adults had received an education.

In the early 1990s, Ameropa started its partnership with Mãe Luíza, a community of about 15,000 people in the city of Natal, Brazil. The initiative of Padre Sabino, backed by supporters from Brazil, Germany and Switzerland, tried to realize a holistic project, based on the priorities expressed by the community. The Centro Sócio, a community association founded in 1983, implemented projects to cover the basic human needs like reducing child mortality, providing access to water and electricity, basic education, housing and, last, but not least, the needs of the elderly. This first phase lasted ca. 20 years. In the second phase, which is still ongoing today, the spiritual needs of the community are being addressed: leisure, sports and culture. (See Historical Milestones, pp. 106–109). It includes the Arena do Morro gymnasium, a center for sports and culture that was built by the architects Herzog & de Meuron, and the Espaço Livre Music School.

Since 2009, the Foundation has also been active with a microcredit loan fund in Kamwokya, a slum of ca. 35,000 people in the capital of Uganda, Kampala. After seeing the positive impact of social infrastructures in Mãe Luíza, the Foundation decided to extend its activities in Kamwokya and invest in the building of social infrastructure, in the same way as in Brazil. An extended playground and community hall, which will offer a variety of possible activities, were designed by Kéré Architecture and are presently being built. The projected completion and inauguration is for 2022.

Friends of Mãe Luíza

In 1986, Loyse Raboud of Switzerland did a one-year internship in Mãe Luíza. She came to Brazil to collaborate on projects with her cousin Jean-Joseph Raboud and his wife Elisabeth Raboud. At that time, she met and married Ion de Andrade. Together, they continued to work at the Centro Sócio with Padre Sabino Gentili.

As friends and family of Loyse got to know the work of the Centro Sócio, they began to hold events in support of its efforts.

In 1995, they decided to establish the Association of Friends of Mãe Luíza to encourage contact and gatherings between very different realities, promote interaction and cultural exchanges, as well as financially support the ongoing activities of the Centro Sócio. The non-profit association closely follows the activities carried out by Centro Sócio and is delighted by the progress it has made thus far.

Over time, bonds of friendship and solidarity were established. Today, association President Nathalie Nicollerat works with a committee of nine, along with volunteers who collaborate in carrying out the association's various activities that include annual gatherings, the Kite Festival held every other year, and the twice-yearly publication of a newsletter distributed to friends to spread the word about the work of the association and the Centro Sócio.

Germany

Penzberg Partnerschaft Mãe Luíza e.V.

The cornerstone of the partnership was laid in 1983, when Padre Sabino, then a young parish vicar in Mãe Luíza, and the former Penzberg parish priest Konrad Albrecht met and became friends. They both dedicated themselves to addressing the needs and

270

concerns of their parishes and to overcoming the existential problems of the people there while giving dignity and hope to those on the margins of society.

As early as 1983, the "Amigos de Sabino" started thinking about how they could support Sabino's work and they thus joined the pioneers of the "Eine Welt Läden" fair trade shops of that era. They asked those in charge in Mãe Luíza to have people there craft simple children's toys to be sold in Penzberg. In time, the shop needed an official sponsor, so the Partnership Group was founded in the parish in 1987.

Intense contacts were soon forged between Penzberg and Mãe Luíza, with mutual visits and young people from Germany traveling to Brazil do a voluntary social year. The "Eine Welt Laden" could finally be opened in 1990 and a supporting association founded. Annual events like Brazil Day and Gospel Night were launched. In 1995, a large group of staff from Mãe Luíza was invited to Germany for the first time. In 2005, on the occasion of World Youth Day in Cologne, a group of ten young people from Mãe Luíza were able to spend two weeks in Penzberg. Since 2011, Gisela Matschl, successor to Joachim Keller as chairperson of the association, has ensured that the partnership is kept alive. Regular visits are organized to share news of the development of Mãe Luíza with the residents of Penzberg.

Eggenthal – Brazil Aid

During preparations for First Communion in 1991, the parish of St. Afra in the German town of Eggenthal came up with the idea of involving the children in a development aid project. The children would then be able to experience helping and sharing firsthand. Johanna Steidele put the parish in contact with the "Amigos de Sabino."

What began at that time has now become a tradition: Every year, the First Communion children and their parents watch a film about the work in Mãe Luíza and then make Easter candles and palm bundles. The children joyfully sell these palm bunches from door to door to raise funds for Mãe Luíza. The proceeds go to the Centro

Sócio, as do the profits from the sale of handicrafts on the patron saint's day. Concerts are also held in the nearby Maria Seelenberg chapel in aid of Mãe Luíza.

Whenever a visit is organized by the Penzberg Partnerschaft Mãe Luíza e.V., the supporters from Eggenthal are always eager to join in.

Parish of St. Michael, Kochel – Partnerschaft Mãe Luíza

In 2003, the first building block was laid for a partnership between the parish of St. Michael in Kochel and Mãe Luíza. During a project with confirmands, Joachim Keller (then chairman of the Partnerschaft Mãe Luíza e.V.) spoke so enthusiastically about the cooperation with Padre Sabino Gentili and about the different projects in Mãe Luíza that the mission committee in Kochel became interested in supporting Padre Sabino in his work.

A slide show about Mãe Luíza and Padre Sabino was first presented to the altar servers at St. Michael, and afterwards the proceeds from the church carol singers were donated to Brazil. The partnership with Mãe Luíza was also addressed as young people prepared for their First Communion and Confirmation. This has been repeated annually since then.

Personal contact with Padre Sabino and later Padre Robério and various employees of the Centro Sócio has strengthened and consolidated this partnership, as is evident from the lovingly prepared excursions and German-Brazilian church services.

Biographies

Paulo Lins was born in Rio de Janeiro on June 11, 1958. He is a poet, novelist and screenwriter for film and television, and a lecturer in Portuguese Language and Brazilian Literature at the Federal University of Rio de Janeiro. His widely acclaimed novel *Cidade de Deus* (translated into English by Alison Entrekin as *City of God*) was published in 1997. The 2002 film adaptation by Fernando Meirelles was nominated for four Academy Awards. Paulo Lins spent his childhood and youth in the Cidade de Deus community, on the outskirts of Rio de Janeiro, where his prize-winning novel is set. His novel *Desde que o samba é samba* (*Since Samba is Samba,* 2012) explores the history of popular music in early 20th century Rio de Janeiro. His writing has been translated into many languages.

Ion de Andrade is a pediatrician, epidemiologist and researcher at the Rio Grande do Norte School of Public Health. He is the current vice-president of the Centro Sócio of Mãe Luíza.

Tomislav Dushanov is an architect. He studied at Harvard Graduate School of Design and is currently an associate at Herzog & de Meuron. With more than 18 years of experience, he has led and completed architectural projects in Spain, France, Brazil, Russia, the UK, and Switzerland. Dushanov was project director for the Arena do Morro. Born in Bulgaria in 1970, he currently lives in Basel, Switzerland.

Nicole Miescher was raised in Switzerland and studied cinematography at the Institut de Hautes Études Cinematographiques (IDHEC) in Paris, as well as photography at CCA in Oakland, California. She managed a screw factory in France and was managing director of Ameropa AG. She is co-founder of the Ameropa Foundation and served as its president until 2019.

Lars Müller is a publisher and graphic designer. In 1982, he launched his studio and one year later, published his first book. As Lars Müller Publishers, he has produced more than 800 titles in the fields of architecture, design, photography, art and society. He has taught at various universities in Europe and the United States.

Herzog & de Meuron was founded in Basel in 1978 and is led by Jacques Herzog and Pierre Meuron together with senior partners Christine Binswanger, Ascan Mergenthaler, Stefan Marbach, Esther Zumsteg and Jason Frantzen. The office's work consists of the totality of all projects. They range from small-scale private houses, museums, stadiums, hospitals, laboratories, office and residential buildings, designs of public places and squares to urban planning and territorial visions.

The **ETH Studio Basel** (1999–2018) was founded by Jacques Herzog and Pierre de Meuron, Roger Diener and Marcel Meili. Until its closure, it pursued an international research program on the contemporary city and the process of transformation in the urban context. All projects are documented in individual publications.

Loyse Raboud de Andrade is a social worker who specializes in gerontology. She directs the Espaço Solidário, Mãe Luíza's eldercare center.

Dulce Bentes is a professor in the Department of Architecture at the Federal University of Rio Grande do Norte in Natal, Brazil.

Mô Bleeker is an anthropologist, specializing in political transitions, development, and humanitarian issues. She has spent several decades working in a variety of environments affected by violence, war, or in transition from authoritarian to democratic regimes. Often acting as a mediator, she specializes in issues of participation, dealing with the legacy of atrocities from the past and the prevention of those in the future.

Robério Camilo da Silva was born in the city of Poço Branco, Rio Grande do Norte, Brazil, in 1959. He holds a master's in Biblical theory, is a Bible teacher, and is president of the Centro Sócio. He lives in the Mãe Luíza neighborhood of Natal, Rio Grande do Norte.

Edilsa Gadelha is an educator. She directs the Espaço Livre preschool and is a member of the Centro Sócio council.

Jacques Herzog studied architecture at the Swiss Federal Institute of Technology (ETH Zurich). Together with Pierre de Meuron, he established Herzog & de Meuron in Basel in 1978. He has been a visiting professor at Harvard University, a professor at ETH Zürich and co-founder of ETH Studio Basel Contemporary City Institute.

Erminia Maricato is a Brazilian architect and urban planner, and a retired full professor from the University of São Paulo. She has held posts in both the São Paulo city government and the Brazilian federal government. Maricato formulated the proposal for establishment of the Ministry of Cities where she served as deputy minister.

Ascan Mergenthaler is a senior partner at Herzog & de Meuron. He has directed the completion of several international projects, including the de Young Museum in San Francisco, the Tate Modern Project in London, and the Elbphilharmonie in Hamburg. Mergenthaler was partner-in-charge for the Arena do Morro gymnasium.

Pierre de Meuron studied architecture at ETH Zurich. Together with Jacques Herzog, he established Herzog & de Meuron in Basel in 1978. He has been visiting professor at Harvard University, a professor at ETH Zürich and co-founder of ETH Studio Basel Contemporary City Institute.

Verner Monteiro is an assistant professor in the Department of Architecture of the Federal University of Rio Grande do Norte. He is also a professor at the Federal Institute of Rio Grande do Norte.

Raymund Ryan is an architectural curator and critic. Born in Cork, Ireland, he has twice served as Irish Commissioner for the Venice Biennale. Since 2003, he has been curator of the Heinz Architectural Center at the Carnegie Museum of Art in Pittsburgh, PA, USA.

Andrea Lorenzo Scartazzini, born in Basel, Switzerland, where he still lives, is a composer of contemporary classical music. His works include operas, orchestral and chamber music, performed by renowned theatres and orchestras throughout Europe.

Josélia Silva Dos Santos is a history professor and community educator. She directs the Casa Crescer educational center and is a member of the Centro Sócio council.

Nicholas Fox Weber has been running the Josef and Anni Albers Foundation for over 40 years and is the founder and president of Le Korsa, a non-profit that works in the areas of medicine, education, and culture in rural Senegal. He has written 16 books and contributed to the *The New York Times, Le Monde, Vogue* and *The New Yorker* in addition to other publications.

274

It has been a fulfilling opportunity to be one of the many collaboration partners in the ongoing transformation of Mãe Luíza. This project is a testament to the value of patience, persistence and determination, and the impact and success that can ensue in a long-term community building project.

We are committed to continuing our work, and are looking forward to sharing the learnings and the successes of this project with other communities in Natal, Brazil and throughout the World, as in the case of Kamwokya, Uganda, where we have been active in various projects since 2011 and are now in the middle of building a sports and community center, designed by Francis Kéré.

Ameropa Foundation
Summer 2021

Mãe Luíza
Building Optimism

With the story "Creating a New Sun"
by Paulo Lins

Editors: Ion de Andrade,
Tomislav Dushanov, Nicole Miescher,
Lars Müller
Editorial assistance: Maya Rüegg
Translations (Port.–Engl.):
Diane Grosklaus, Kim Olson
Copyediting and proofreading:
Kim Olson
Design: Integral Lars Müller/
Lars Müller and Ronja Burkard
Lithography: prints professional,
Berlin, Germany
Printing and binding: DZA Druckerei
zu Altenburg, Germany
Paper: Magno Volume, 135 gsm;
Munken Print White, 130 gsm

© 2021 The Ameropa Foundation
and Lars Müller Publishers

"Creating a New Sun": © 2021 Paulo
Lins, by arrangement with Literarische
Agentur Mertin Inh. Nicole Witt e.K.,
Frankfurt am Main, Germany

Lars Müller Publishers is supported
by the Swiss Federal Office of Culture
with a structural contribution for the
years 2021–2024.

Lars Müller Publishers
Zurich, Switzerland
www.lars-mueller-publishers.com

ISBN 978-3-03778-682-6, English
ISBN 978-3-03778-689-5, German

Distributed in North America
by ARTBOOK | D.A.P.
www.artbook.com

Printed in Germany

Image Credits

All photographs © Nicole Miescher
except as indicated below.

p. 78/79, 89, 90, 91, 116 top, 117 top,
119 top, 178
© Copyright unknown

p. 98/99
© Verner Monteiro

p. 100 top left
Região Metropolitana de Natal-
Extremoz: trecho Ponta Negra-
Genipabu

p. 101 bottom, 132 top, 218/219, 220,
221, 224 top, 225 top, 226 bottom,
227/228, 244/45
© Iwan Baan

p. 102 bottom
© Archive Centro Sócio Pastoral

p. 118 bottom
Photo: Igor Jácome/G1.Globo

p. 122, 148, 151, 201
© Raboud

p. 217
© Penzberg

p. 224 bottom
© Tomislav Dushanov

We thank Raymund Ryan for allowing
us to use the title of his exhibition
Building Optimism, which took place
from September 10 through February
13, 2017, at the Heinz Architectural
Center at the Carnegie Museum
of Art in Pittsburgh, PA, USA.